It's a delectable read. Rebecca Yeung is an authentic and powerful storyteller. With *What Rules?*, she provides us with an operating manual for life. I loved how the book ends with an accountability framework that is very easy to follow and implement. I am going to go back to this book frequently to create and enrich my garden of life.

KAWAL PREET,
President, Asia Pacific, Middle East and Africa (AMEA), FedEx

Rebecca's profound and practical insights resonate deeply, providing guidance for realizing your own ambitions while navigating "the rules" amidst all hurdles and un-clarity, especially encountered by minorities like women in STEM and first-generation immigrants such as myself. To highlight favorite passages would risk divulging all the wisdom within the book. It is indeed a treasure trove for those seeking to forge their own authentic leadership sig-nature, fostering an open and inquisitive mindset toward opportunities ahead, and savoring the journey rather than solely fixating on the ultimate destination.

OLI QIRKO,
President, Cambridge Consultants North America

What Rules? Think Differently About Success and Cultivate a Happy Life marks an astonishing chronicle of Rebecca Yeung's life journey of emerging from the most humble beginnings in China to boardrooms of the United States of America. While I was reminded to embrace my strengths and to celebrate the wins, this body of work also provided me with new strategies for enhancing my own personal and professional journey.

RENÉE HORNE,
Chief Marketing & Customer Experience Officer, Chase Auto

In her book, *What Rules? Think Differently About Success and Cultivate a Happy Life,* Rebecca Yeung offers a powerful guide to breaking free from conventional constraints, embracing clarity, and living a purpose-driven life. Having personally met Rebecca at a professional crossroads, her thought-provoking questions helped me uncover clarity and align my strengths with passion, propelling my career path forward. Her teachings are a masterpiece, seamlessly blending meaningful advice with profound wisdom. I highly recommend this book to anyone who feels stuck, misaligned, or yearning for more in their journey toward success and happiness. It's a transformative read, leaving you inspired and empowered to make positive changes in your life.

ANNE MARIE LEAVITT MCDONALD,
CEO, Ammp Growth

In less than the time it takes for dinner and a movie, *What Rules?* evokes, examines, and then dashes every relic of success formulas and provides alternative ways to think about, plan, and capture self-success. To borrow from its core metaphor, *What Rules?* should become bamboo for all.

GLORIA R. BOYLAND,
Fortune 50 Senior Executive, Board Director

With her unique, seamless blend of Eastern and Western wisdom, Rebecca demonstrates how personal and professional disadvantages can be reframed to bring success within reach for anyone. An empowering read!

MAGGIE VAN DE GRIEND,
Founder & Managing Principal, Sokrates Partners LLC

A thought-provoking read for people at all stages of their lives, *What Rules?* includes so many nuggets of wisdom. Rebecca's life experiences (from childhood to corporate board rooms), and her honesty about overcoming life's challenges and anxieties are inspiring. Her approach of continuously evaluating "rules" to live by, and "rules" to ignore, is a lesson for all, women and men.

SEV MCMURTRY,
Corporate Vice President, FedEx

What Rules? Think Differently About Success and Cultivate a Happy Life provides a unique and insightful perspective on resilience and thriving both in your personal and professional life. Rebecca's story is uplifting and encouraging. It is joyfully told and offers valuable wisdom to help you live into your full potential.

DONALD COMER,
Vice President—Decision Science and Analytics, FedEx

Rebecca is an amazing businesswoman, a great friend, and a delightful mix of contradictions. She is a marketing person with a liberal arts degree who leads advanced technology. A person with dyslexia who aced a language exam to get into college. A Chinese-American woman who has risen to corporate success deep in the American heartland. *What Rules?* does an excellent job of distilling her life experiences into a series of easily digestible lessons for anyone to follow, and these truths that it articulates are ones that I hold dear to my own career.

HAOMIAO HUANG, PHD,
Partner & Co-Founder, Matter Venture Partners

Rebecca's story truly inspired me to think differently about my career and realize what's most important along this journey called life.

CHRIS WINTON,
Senior Vice President Human Resources, Comcast

As an Asian-American woman in business, Rebecca's voice and perspective are one we don't hear from enough. I've had the pleasure of experiencing her wisdom and warmth personally, and I'm glad that so many more people can now receive the benefit of her insights through this delightful book. It's a well-written, snappy read.

LYDIA THE

The stories from Rebecca's personal journey and non-linear career path resonated deeply with me. This book is a must-read for people who feel like they are stuck in their current positions, their careers have stagnated, or are looking for a way to live a fully integrated life. *What Rules? Think Differently About Success and Cultivate a Happy Life* is like a personal executive/life coach, packed with unconventional advice and actionable tools to transform oneself.

EMILY CHHAN, MBA,
District Manager, FedEx

In *What Rules?*, Rebecca demonstrates that to be successful and happy, we first must dare to be ourselves. In this book, she shares with us the lessons learned and the wisdom gathered in her life through her genuine voice. Rebecca's inspiring journey is like the process of how a pearl is made: painful, but with grit and patience, the result is beautiful and precious. This book is THE BEST gift I can give to my daughters as they sail to college this summer and start writing their own stories and pushing new limits. It also has great healing power for those of us amazing professionals to find encouragement and guidance. Rebecca's story changed the dynamic for us in that it's no longer the question of *What can I do?* but *What do I want to do?*

YAPEI ALICE HONG,
Mother, Sister, Mountain Bike Coach and Working Professional

An inspirational story of resilience and fulfillment. I found myself connecting with Rebecca's journey of defining her pathway throughout the book. Enjoy the read!

RAMONA HOOD,
President and CEO at FedEx Custom Critical,
Independent Director

As an executive woman in the fast-paced tech industry, I found Rebecca Yeung's book to be deeply grounding and a stark reminder that we have the power to shift our mindset to align with personal values and goals. Full of practical advice, I plan to use Rebecca's book and worksheets as a reference guide for years to come.

CYNTHIA KWON,
SVP Product, Stack AV

What Rules? empowers us to stop stifling our growth and happiness by confining ourselves to restrictive parameters others have established, and to instead carve out our own unique paths. Author Rebecca Yeung adeptly combines vivid metaphors, relatable anecdotes, contemporary psychological theories, and time-tested wisdom from both the East and West to enlighten and entertain without ever preaching. In lieu of tossing out the well-meaning but ultimately unhelpful generalities that one might find in a tabloid horoscope, this captivating read delves into specific issues and techniques. Readers are encouraged to ask themselves tantalizing questions and formulate concrete plans based on our candid replies. What Rules? is a sage, hopeful gem that inspires all of us to redefine who we are, what we really want our lives to look like, and how to fulfill those dreams by shaking off the shackles of the unwritten yet no less binding rules that limit us all.

BETH VANDERSLICE,
Partner, Trewstar Corporate Board Services

I dedicate this book to my amazing parents, my loving husband, my two wonderful daughters, and my thoughtful friends, mentors, and sponsors. You inspire me to overcome barriers and follow my own path to cultivate a happy, fulfilling life.

WHAT RULES?

Think Differently About Success and Cultivate a Happy Life

REBECCA YEUNG

What Rules? Think Differently About
Success and Cultivate a Happy Life

Copyright © 2024 Rebecca Yeung

Published by StoryBuilders Press
Illustrations by Abby Truitt

Ebook: 978-1-954521-33-9
Hardcover: 978-1-954521-34-6
Paperback: 978-1-954521-35-3

TABLE OF CONTENTS

FOREWORD

I n my years guiding leaders across the globe, I've encountered stories of grit, innovation, and the unyielding spirit of those who dare to dream. Among these, Rebecca Yeung's journey emerges as a beacon of resilience and the relentless pursuit of excellence.

Born into challenging circumstances, Rebecca's path to becoming a technology innovation leader at a Fortune 50 company is nothing short of remarkable. Her story, however, is more than a series of achievements; it's a testament to the power of embracing your unique perspective and experiences.

Rebecca's narrative challenges conventional wisdom, breaking ceilings of glass—and bamboo—to reveal the essence of true leadership. It's not merely about the positions we hold, but about how we navigate our journey, the principles we uphold, and the impact we create.

Through her lens, we see the world differently—a world where being different can be your greatest asset, opening doors to endless possibilities.

What makes Rebecca's story compelling is not just her ascent in Corporate America but the profound insights and lessons she learned along the way. From leveraging her background as a strength to redefining success on her own terms, Rebecca's journey inspires us as readers to reflect on our own paths and the so-called rules we live by.

This book is an invitation to explore Rebecca's world—a world where barriers are meant to be broken, and the status quo is continuously challenged. *What Rules?* captures the essence of her approach to life and leadership, urging us to question our limitations and redefine our potential.

As you turn these pages, let Rebecca's story inspire you to explore the power of your unique narrative and how it can shape your understanding of success. Welcome to a journey of discovery, transformation, and the courage to chart your own course.

GAYLE GRADER

Executive, Career, and Leadership Coach, Business Advisor
Senior Director, MIT Sloan School of Management,
Executive Career Development

CHAPTER ONE

THE POWER BENEATH THE SURFACE

In a small Chinese village nestled between rolling hills and vibrant meadows, there lived a farmer whose spirit matched the vastness of the land he called home. His weathered hands were a testament to years of toiling under the scorching sun, yet his heart remained filled with an unwavering determination and an unyielding belief in the power of nature.

One spring morning, as a gentle breeze caressed the farmer's face, he was holding a tiny bamboo seed in his hand. With a soft smile, the farmer set out to create the perfect environment for his precious seed. He tilled the earth, removing stones and smoothing the soil's cradle-like embrace. Tenderly, he nestled the seed in the ground, as if entrusting his dreams to the very heart of the earth.

From long experience, he knew that this was just the beginning.

The farmer greeted each new day with a resolute spirit, donning his worn hat and picking up his trusty watering can. Like a symphony conductor, he orchestrated the dance of the water droplets nourishing the earth. With every drop, he reveled in the notion that he was nurturing a miracle in the making.

Days passed, and the seed lay still, hidden beneath the soil's embrace. One bright morning, the farmer arrived in the field, and to his delight, he found a small, slender shoot emerging from the soil's nurturing embrace, reaching skyward like an artist's brush stroke upon a canvas. He greeted the new growth with gratitude and was inspired in his devotion.

Day after day, for two months, he visited the field and found that the new shoots had grown from a single inch to two and then to two feet tall. He watched the canes thicken and strengthen to support their growth and the leaves stretch outward to catch the sunlight and create the nutrients the plant needed. The farmer's excitement and enthusiasm grew in proportion to the plant's development.

And then, the growth stopped.

The sun still shone, and the farmer still watered and tended the plant, but nothing above the surface changed.

Many would have faltered, questioning the plant's future, but not the farmer. He knew that greatness took time, that nature had a rhythm of its own. So he continued his daily ritual, unyielding in his belief even when there appeared to be no growth.

He knew that greatness took time, that nature had a rhythm of its own.

As the second year dawned, the farmer's perseverance was tested. He knew this would happen, but doubt still whispered in his ear, attempting to extinguish the fire of his dreams. But he turned a deaf ear to its sly voice, for he understood that nature's most precious gifts were bestowed upon those who stayed the course.

Undeterred by the passage of time, the farmer continued to tend to his bamboo. He whispered words of encouragement, sharing stories of magnificent bamboo forests that once thrived in the heart of the land.

The years rolled by, and as the third year slipped into its autumn, the farmer stood at the crossroads of hope and doubt. Shadows danced around him, casting doubts upon his unwavering faith. He could have turned away, abandoning the plant to its fate, but that was not the way of the farmer.

As the fourth year arrived, and spring's first warm breath filtered through the awakening world, the farmer's eyes widened in awe as he witnessed the beginning of what he had nurtured and hoped for. He sat down beside the small plant and watched as its leaves shuddered in the wind, the cane grew taller, and the new shoots emerged from the ground, right before his eyes!

While the plant appeared to have lain dormant for years, below the surface, it was silently weaving a complex tapestry. Deep underneath the earth, a network of roots, strong and intricate, had been taking shape, anchoring the tree to the very soul of the land to support the growth that was to come.

> *While the plant appeared to have lain dormant for years, below the surface, it was silently weaving a complex tapestry.*

With each passing day, the plant grew taller, wider, and stronger at an astonishing rate. The canes extended like a telescope toward the sky, the shoots sprang up in every direction, and the leaves branched outward and created shade below. Word of the farmer's incredible seed spread like wildfire, drawing villagers from all around. They marveled at the bamboo, their eyes wide with wonder, as they watched the small plant transform into an extraordinary grove in just weeks. The farmer's eyes twinkled as he replied that the bamboo's journey from seed to shoot to tree was a testament to resilience, patience, and unwavering faith.

He knew that the secret wasn't what they could see, but rather, what they couldn't see—the magic that happened below the soil.

Waiting for a Breakthrough in Life

As we consider the incredible journey of the bamboo tree, we can't help but see echoes of our own lives. Like that tiny seed patiently growing beneath the surface, we too encounter moments when it feels like we're stuck below the surface, longing to break free and grow into our full potential. Kept in a dirty, dark, and cramped place, we don't like that feeling of "stuckness" and want it to end.

> *Like that tiny seed patiently growing beneath the surface, we too encounter moments when it feels like we're stuck below the surface, longing to break free and grow into our full potential.*

During these times of uncertainty and feeling stuck, it's tempting to believe that you're trapped in an endless loop or that your progress is halted at a dead-end road. Sometimes your growth seems to stall, and doubt begins to blur your vision of the limitless possibilities that lie just beyond your reach. You feel like the perpetual underdog, always scratching and clawing your way toward success that you see around you but constantly remains just beyond your reach. You may feel like the ugly duckling, finding yourself sticking out in painful ways and unable to figure out your place, or even just how to fit in.

Indecision and fear of change can keep you from growing too. You're overwhelmed by choices, afraid of making the wrong decision. It's like you're frozen, unable to move forward and embrace new opportunities for growth and happiness.

And then there's that feeling of emptiness when you're not fulfilled personally. You find yourself disconnected from your passions and lacking a sense of purpose. It's like the joy and excitement you used to have has faded away, leaving you searching for something more meaningful.

If you or someone close to you has ever felt stuck in a dead-end job that offers no room for growth or advancement, you probably know it can be frustrating. It can make you feel like you're going nowhere. Your talents and ambitions go unnoticed, and you're left yearning for opportunities that seem out of reach.

Stagnant in Corporate America

Think about an ambitious professional who has set their sights on climbing the corporate ladder. With determination and a hunger for success, they have dedicated themselves to acquiring new skills, expanding their knowledge, and seizing every opportunity that comes their way. However, despite their relentless efforts, they haven't witnessed any significant progress in their career advancement for what feels like an eternity.

Even though they couldn't see the immediate results, they were unknowingly preparing for a breakthrough, building a reservoir of expertise and resilience.

Days turn into weeks, weeks into months, and months into years, and yet, the aspiring manager finds themselves stuck in the same position with no signs of upward mobility. They begin to question their abilities and wonder if their dreams of reaching higher levels of responsibility and influence are merely wishful thinking. The absence of promotions and the perceived lack of growth make them believe that perhaps this stagnant state is their destiny and that they have reached the limits of their professional journey.

In this moment of frustration, it's easy for the aspiring manager to accept this situation as the ultimate reality. They start to settle, convincing themselves that this is all there is to their career trajectory. Doubt seeps into their thoughts, whispering discouragement and pushing them to abandon their ambitious aspirations.

But think back to the tale of the bamboo and the farmer. Growth is not always apparent on the surface, and progress can often be concealed from view. Just like the bamboo tree's roots, silently weaving an intricate network underground, the aspiring manager's growth may be happening in imperceptible ways.

Maybe they don't know that every project tackled, every challenge faced, and every skill acquired is contributing to their professional foundation. Even though they couldn't see the immediate results, they were unknowingly preparing for a breakthrough, building a reservoir of expertise and resilience.

That, in a nutshell, describes my own experience back in the early 2000s as a new employee of FedEx. I had dreams of growing as far and as fast as I could within the organization. But my roots go back farther than that— all the way to a small village in China, much like the bamboo farmer's village.

A Chinese Cinderella Beginning

The first six years of my life were spent in a small rural village in Changzhou, China, where I was raised by my aunt while my parents were assigned by the government to work in two separate cities. Each of them made only an equivalent of twelve dollars per month, so they couldn't afford to pay a nanny to keep me. Instead, they sent me to live with my aunt. Our home was a simple one-room hut with a straw roof and a dirt floor, just like all my neighbors. We did not have electricity, and we drew water from the village well for washing, drinking, and cooking. Luxuries were things like plentiful rain and fish caught from the creek for lunch, not cars or refrigeration. In fact, I didn't experience air-conditioning until I was in my early twenties.

Life in the village revolved around a close-knit community that shared a deep love for one another. When someone needed help, others were quick to offer assistance. The nearest market was two miles away, so we grew what we ate, and if it didn't grow, we didn't eat—except for the kindness of our neighbors. If someone had plenty, others were invited to share it. I could show up at anyone's home at mealtime, and they would feed me as if I were a member of their family, and we would do the same.

Formal education was unavailable, but my innate curiosity drove me to learn organically through play, exploration, and experimentation. With no money available for toys, my friends and I ingeniously fashioned playthings out of broken pottery, sticks, and dirt, inventing new games and playing old favorites. We especially loved to play hide-and-seek, covering ourselves with straw and hiding behind the chickens. No one liked to search for someone hiding behind the chickens because of the strong ammonia smell that wafted from their coop.

That may sound unappealing, but it's all my neighbors and I knew at the time, and we were content and happy. This was a time of my life when, like the bamboo seed, my potential was newly sown and felt plentiful. I was unencumbered by social conventions, free to grow, roam and explore, and play and learn as I pleased. Free from discrimination, judgment, and comparison. Free to try new things (and fail), constantly supported by genuinely kind people.

When I was seven, my parents were assigned to new jobs in Shanghai, and our family was reunited. Though I was sad to leave the village, the prospect of our reunion filled me with hope and excitement.

But the transition to city life was challenging. The transition from informal learning to formal education was jarring, to say the least. For the first time, I was surrounded by judgment, comparison, and expectations that I was well aware I failed to meet.

I found it hard to fit in at school. My teachers called me "dumb" because of my undiagnosed dyslexia, and my appearance, with darker skin and a slightly chubbier frame than what was culturally considered to be "pretty" in China, contributed to my being treated as an outsider by my peers too.

In China, academic performance tests determine the schools students attend. These assignments are perceived as strong indicators of a child's future success in Chinese society. When I was twelve years old, I tested into the lowest-performing middle school, which could have shamed my family.

My mom sat me down for a heart-to-heart conversation, saying, "You're very talented. I believe in you, but you have to believe in yourself. You have two choices: you either accept your current situation and remain miserable, or you decide to fight for something better with your whole heart. That's the only way you will be happy in your life."

> *You either accept your current situation and remain miserable, or you decide to fight for something better with your whole heart.*

That moment changed everything for me. She could have been disappointed or ashamed of me, but instead, she believed in me. She offered me support. She saw my potential and believed in my ability to shape a future for myself beyond my present expectations. Her encouragement was profound, but her words also affirmed in me that I had the agency and ability to change my own destiny.

It was as if that little bamboo seed had its first sprout spring up from the dirt. I determined then and there that I would fight—with my whole heart—for a better life. Since that conversation with my mom in 1984, I have been consistently pushing forward, never entertaining the idea that any limitations could hold me back.

Simply put—on that day, I began to *think differently*, and it has made all the difference.

> *Simply put—on that day, I began to think differently, and it has made all the difference.*

In fact, I believe that is the true essence of a fulfilling life, and it is what we will examine more closely in the chapters to come. We will explore why some people reach a plateau in their lives and careers and stall out, while others experience potential growth like the bamboo seed breaking through and flourishing at great heights. We will challenge conventional wisdom and invert the truths hidden within the seemingly positive rules we've come to unconsciously believe in.

My hope is to challenge your thinking, spark curiosity, and inspire you to question the hidden constraints that may be holding you back. Prepare to explore a world of transformative ideas and unexpected revelations and embrace fresh perspectives. Like the persistent, tenacious, and resilient way of the bamboo tree, you will discover how to break free of your limitations and nurture your life to its fullest potential.

CHAPTER TWO

THE FRUSTRATION OF STAGNATION

I magine you took a trip to China, and as part of your travel itinerary, you spent time visiting Yibin City in southwest China's Sichuan Province, which has the largest bamboo forest in the world. As you stand amid the sprawling bamboo forest, you are visually overwhelmed by the grandeur of hundreds of millions of bamboo trees covering twenty-seven mountains and more than five hundred peaks—it's simply stunning. Hoping to capture a memento of this magical place, you purchase a package of bamboo seeds to bring home with you and plant in your backyard.

But nobody told you about the slow growth process that the seeds must undergo.

Excitedly, you return home and find the perfect spot in the corner of your yard. You carefully plant the bamboo seeds, imagining your own peaceful, emerald-green corner of the world. With great anticipation, you do everything a good gardener would do: watering diligently, fertilizing the soil, and meticulously weeding the area. And then you wait, with bated breath, for signs of growth and transformation.

Now, be honest. What would you think or do when a month later, after countless hours of tender care, you see no growth? Three months later? *A year later?*

Would you still be enthusiastically and patiently tending the seed patch, or would doubt begin to creep into your mind?

What went wrong? Were the seeds defective? Did I make a mistake?

I'm sure you understand the connection I'm making. At some point in your professional journey, you will likely reach a point where you feel like you're making no progress. You're stuck. Despite countless hours devoted to learning, networking, and personal growth, reaching your desired destination seems elusive.

I had been with FedEx for ten years, and while I moved positions in different areas of the company, they were all lateral moves. I had broad exposure to different fields but never advanced in any of them. Watching my colleagues advance into management positions and move up the corporate ladder inspired me to take action so I wouldn't be left behind.

So I worked harder.

I set SMART (specific, measurable, achievable, relevant, and time-bound) goals for myself and the projects I worked on. Like a sponge, I learned as much as I could about all aspects of the business—such as marketing, product development, e-commerce, customer experience, supply chain, operations, and quality—and adopted new strategies for leadership and communications.

Like most women, I thought that if I demonstrated my expertise and commitment through integrity, good decisions, and hard work, someone would notice and award me with the promotion I desired.[1]

But when the opportunities came, I was passed over.

The rejection stung. I began to second-guess my choices. I worried that the time I had spent focusing on my family in the early years of my career had permanently hampered my ability to achieve my career goals. I wondered about my place and future at the company. The negative responses to this experience that I had seen were for an employee to either inappropriately lash out and damage their own reputation, quietly assume they had reached their highest potential and stop trying for more, or simply leave the company.

I just didn't believe that was for me.

Traditional Chinese wisdom offers insights into the experience of feeling stuck in one's career and provides guidance on navigating this challenging phase. One such concept is the principle of *wu wei*, which translates to "effortless action" or "non-doing." It stems from Taoism, an ancient Chinese philosophy emphasizing harmony with nature and the flow of life.

According to the principle of wu wei, when faced with obstacles or feeling stuck, you are encouraged to embrace a more relaxed and intuitive approach. Rather than exerting excessive effort or forcing outcomes, it suggests aligning oneself with the natural rhythms of life and allowing things to unfold organically. It entails recognizing that some circumstances are beyond our control and that by surrendering to the natural course of events, we can find greater ease and clarity.

I had tried to hustle and grind my way to the top, but it produced no traction for me and only left me frustrated and confused. But I also couldn't just let my dream slip away. I didn't believe my career journey was over, but I also saw clearly that not every step of it was under my control. Unwilling to surrender my ambition, I decided I needed direction and clarity. Intuitively, I combined the wisdom of the East and West and began the process of growth, though no one else could see it yet.

Feeling Stuck

Maybe you have also experienced the profound impact of feeling stuck, whether it's in your career or other areas of your life. It begins with a sense of unfulfillment and a nagging lack of passion. The once vibrant and purposeful days gradually transform into a monotonous routine void of excitement and meaning. Tasks that once sparked joy and held deep significance lose their luster, becoming mundane and uninspiring. A persistent dissatisfaction settles in, casting a shadow over your every move.

As this subtle feeling of being trapped intensifies, frustration starts to seep into your consciousness like an unwelcome guest. The work that once fascinated and engaged you now feels unchallenging and devoid of meaning, leaving you disengaged and lacking motivation. It's as if a spark within you has dimmed, and you find yourself yearning to reignite the flames of inspiration.

This state of feeling stuck takes a toll not only on your external circumstances but also on your mental and emotional well-being. The mounting pressure of unfulfilled desires and unrealized potential and the absence of progress begin to weigh heavily on your shoulders. Stress, anxiety, and even bouts of depression start to infiltrate your daily life, draining your energy and impacting your overall sense of happiness. The once joyful pursuit of your work now feels like an uphill battle, testing your resilience and leaving you desperately searching for a way to reclaim your passion.

As this feeling of being stuck lingers, self-doubt starts to creep into your thoughts, planting seeds of uncertainty and making you question your abilities and worth. You find yourself wondering if you possess the necessary skills and qualities to achieve your goals after all. Further, this self-doubt extends beyond your career, seeping into other crucial areas of your life. The mere thought of taking risks or seizing new opportunities becomes daunting as fear and uncertainty tighten their grip, leaving you hesitant and reluctant to step outside your comfort zone. The fear of failure looms large, causing you to shrink back instead of embracing the growth that awaits.

While those around you appear to be making strides and climbing the ladder of success, you can't help but feel left behind, a silent observer of their progress. It's disheartening to witness your colleagues advancing in their careers while you remain stagnant, stuck in a seemingly unending loop of unfulfillment. The lack of momentum fuels a growing sense of restlessness within you, igniting a deep-seated desire for change and a yearning to break free from the confines of your current circumstances.

Can you relate to any of this? Do you find yourself nodding in recognition, knowing all too well the pain and frustration of feeling stuck?

Statistically Speaking

It is also important to highlight that forward momentum (or lack thereof) is not always solely influenced by our internal perceptions of obstacles. Statistically speaking, there are some actual hurdles women in the workplace face that may exacerbate the condition of being stuck.

Women in the workplace are often subjected to different standards than their male counterparts

For professional women in America, there is a pervasive phenomenon known as the "broken rung." This term alludes to the difficulty many women encounter when seeking to advance their careers up the corporate ladder from entry-level positions to managers. This "broken rung" can be a real hindrance to women's success, and it is caused by a few significant factors, foremost of which is a lack of diversity in all levels of management.

According to management consulting company McKinsey & Company's "Women in the Workplace 2022" report, for every one hundred men hired and promoted to manager, only eighty-seven women are hired and promoted. For minority women, that number is even worse: just eighty-two women of color are hired and promoted, despite their ambition and desire to advance.[2]

Women in the workplace are often subjected to different standards than their male counterparts. They face scrutiny for how they look and if they dress too femininely—or not femininely enough. They are encouraged to display assertiveness yet can be unjustly viewed as aggressive, self-promoting, domineering, or lacking a collaborative mindset if they are. These implicit standards and expectations can create a confining, confusing environment for women, leaving them uncertain of the best course of action to realize their aspirations.

Women are heavily socialized to adhere to the rules and strive to please others. They often consciously or unconsciously subscribe to the idea that their dedication, skill, and competencies will be demonstrated through their diligent efforts, ultimately leading to supervisor recognition and promotion or, at the very least, equal recognition to their male counterparts.[3]

Unfortunately, women are also more likely than men to have another coworker take credit for their work, be mistaken for junior employees, have unclear evaluation standards, and have fewer mentors and support.[4] These dynamics can lead to overwork and underappreciation, which ultimately creates burnout, and burnout affects more women than men.[5]

Women in every culture are also responsible for carrying a large portion of the mental, physical, and emotional load of the home and family even while pursuing a career. Data shows that more than half of women at all levels of management are also primarily responsible for child-rearing and housework.[6]

While these cultural challenges can seem daunting though, they are just that: challenges. And they will only keep you stuck if you allow them to.

It's Time to Grow

Feeling stuck may seem like a dead-end situation, but it can also be a time of unprecedented yet hidden growth. After experiencing the disappointment of being passed over for the initial promotion to manager, I found myself slipping into a sense of stagnation that permeated nearly every aspect of my life.

But I had two major advantages: I knew about the bamboo, and I believed in wu wei. I understood that while I do not appear to be growing, I may actually be developing those strong foundational roots necessary for my future explosive growth.

Determined to nurture that unseen growth, I was eager to learn what I needed to do to grow.

The first thing I did was to lean into my strength of curiosity. I spoke to my director at that time and asked him what he felt was holding me back from advancement. I welcomed his perspective on my skills and career, and I shared with him my ambitions. He and I had a three-hour conversation about my strengths and weaknesses. He asked questions about what I thought made a good leader and offered his own insights.

One eye-popping moment for me was when he asked me why I wanted to become a manager. My answers were, "I am smart," "I work hard," "My friends have moved up, and I want to be successful also."

Much like the bamboo, being stuck is actually an opportunity for a growth phase.

He looked at me with a chuckle and told me, "You have all the wrong reasons to be a manager. Being a leader is nothing about you but everything about the people you lead. The best leader is one who brings out the best in other people."

I left that conversation motivated and inspired to action.

After our conversation, I became fascinated about leadership and started learning. I read many books on leadership, like *What Got You Here Won't Get You There* by Marshall Goldsmith and *Start with Why* by Simon Sinek. I intensely watched the good leaders around me for the traits and skills they had that separated them from the others. Conversely, I also formed a habit of noting down bad leadership behaviors and things that I should avoid. I sought to truly understand the qualities of good leadership better, not just mimic the behaviors. Once I identified a challenge in an area of my leadership skills,

I'd try to absorb as much information about it and seek out mentors in the business who can coach me through.

Much like the bamboo, being stuck is actually an opportunity for a growth phase. In fact, it is the opportune time to nurture the roots that are growing unseen, which will ultimately support your future success. In the upcoming chapters, we will delve further into the concept of reframing our perception of growth and exploring how it can be instrumental in overcoming challenges.

But first, allow me to provide some context as I share more about my journey from a small village in China to the C-Suite of a Fortune 50 company.

CHAPTER THREE

SEEDS OF CHANGE

One cool spring evening when I was ten years old, I stood over our little television set excited to watch my favorite show, and my life changed. I didn't know it at the time, but as I look back, I can see it was that key moment when a tiny seed was planted in me, which would one day produce unstoppable growth.

Our apartment in Shanghai was modest to say the least. With a mere seven square meters (seventy-five square feet) for the three of us to call home, and concrete walls and concrete floor, there was no room for extravagance. We had no air-conditioning to shield us from the heat and humidity of summer and no heat to warm us in the winter. It was a safe place to sleep rather than to spend a lot of free time, with just our beds, a small cooking area, and a simple wash closet tucked away in the corner. One luxury we enjoyed was our ten-inch, black-and-white television perched upon a sturdy shelf.

Color television made its way to China in the 1980s, but it would be many years before we could afford such a lavish upgrade to our basic set. Yet even in the grayscale world of our television, we found joy and entertainment.

This particular evening, as the screen flickered to life, I couldn't believe my eyes—color! Or at least, a facsimile of it. Standing there, I watched it for a while, captivated by the sight before me. Actors appeared in green, red, yellow, and all the colors in between. But as I watched, I began to notice a pattern. The red hues always appeared on the upper-right side, while the green and yellow remained fixed in their designated spots as well. It was then that I realized my mother's creative solution—a touch of her invention and resourcefulness. She had ingeniously affixed color transparencies to the black-and-white screen, giving us a small taste of the vibrant world of color television. It wasn't perfect, but it was mesmerizing.

On another occasion, our lack of storage and shower facilities became a sources of frustration for my mother. In the early 1980s, most apartments in Shanghai didn't have built-in showers. We had to go to public baths every other day, which was inconvenient and had zero privacy. In addition to a shower, we also needed somewhere to store our winter clothes, but in seven square meters, storage and privacy were both in short supply.

But my mother, a radio engineer, was unconvinced that solutions were beyond her reach. One day she came home with a hydraulic saw tool. Undeterred by the concrete wall before her, she fearlessly cut right through it to open up the top of the narrow wall that separated the toilet and bedroom. She lowered a portion of the ceiling over the toilet to create a small storage space for clothes that we could access from the bedroom side.

On the bathroom side, she ran hot and cold water tubes to the top of the lowered ceiling, strategically positioning a pump to create a shower that drained into the toilet below. Although the water flowed hot on one side and cold on the other without mixing, it was a vast improvement over having no shower! My mother had ingeniously found one solution for both problems.

But even if you have numerous resources at your disposal, by thinking creatively about challenges, you gain adaptability, agility, and ultimately, the opportunity for significant future growth.

One gift of not having much is that you are forced to think unconventionally about solving problems. But even if you have numerous resources at your disposal, by thinking creatively about challenges, you gain

29

adaptability, agility, and ultimately, the opportunity for significant future growth. You will even inspire others by your actions, as my mother did for me.

Barriers Are Beginnings

When faced with barriers or adversity, it's easy to succumb to overwhelm or self-doubt. You may be tempted to abandon your goals and dreams altogether because of the roadblocks in your path. You may be tempted to listen to the voices of others around you telling you something is impossible, or just impossible for you.

Since I was a child, I had worked hard to prove myself, because I *had* to work harder than my peers to accomplish the same tasks, but also because my challenges made me feel like I wasn't enough.

When I turned forty, and my career seemingly stalled, these thoughts only magnified in my mind. I felt like I didn't belong, like I was an impostor who had to work harder than everyone else to earn my place.

On the outside, my life and career might have looked relatively calm, but inside, I struggled with doubts. I began to question my path and second-guess my decision to focus on my family in my early career. I wondered if I'd made a misstep by not committing to one specific function in the company because I kept on exploring and learning about the business. I questioned whether this broad exposure and nonlinear path I had chosen during my time at FedEx was actually a road to nowhere.

Maybe you've followed the conventional rules or advice of others your whole professional life but you're still not where you want to be. Perhaps you've exhausted your knowledge and understanding and you're starting to think your rise to the top must end here. Maybe up until

Barriers are only beginnings in disguise.

now, your professional life has been fairly uneventful, and now for the first time, you are encountering friction on your path to success. Or maybe, like me, your journey has been challenging from the start and you're wondering if it's worth pressing on.

I understand the temptation to respond with overwhelm or defeat. In the face of barriers and limitations, it is necessary to think and act differently. Doing so may not be comfortable or easy, but it also will probably not be as hard as you think. Even small acts of creativity can reignite your excitement and turn what looks like barriers into opportunities. Barriers are only beginnings in disguise.

A Foundation of Grit

How do I know? Because I've been there. I've been an underdog my whole life. Poverty, dyslexia, and a language barrier, as well as being a liberal arts major, an immigrant, and a woman, have all made me an underdog at different times. These life situations and circumstances required me to take a different approach. Advantages and opportunities were never handed to me on a silver platter; I had to earn them through hard work and innovation from the very beginning.

Even within my own family, the underdog spirit runs deep. My paternal grandfather, a tenant farmer, perpetually struggled to earn enough money just to pay his rent. He spent his entire life toiling in the fields around the same village, never venturing beyond its boundaries to experience the world outside.

My father, on the other hand, won a college scholarship and was able to leave the village. From him I inherited my love of learning, thoroughness, and another large dose of hard work and creativity. His intelligence and hard work opened the door for his education and career as a marine engineer. Though this offered him some travel and marked a significant step up from his humble upbringing, he never surpassed the position of manager.

Despite the challenges of growing up in a poor, rural village, I was genuinely very happy as a young child, other than the times of hunger I'd experienced. The collective hardships we faced seemed less daunting because we had each other, all sharing the same experiences. These experiences instilled in me the quality of grit and a commitment to the people around me.

Grit refers to when you apply passion and sustained persistence toward a long-term achievement, with no particular

> *"If you don't like something, change it."*

concern for rewards or recognition along the way. Survival itself was our primary objective. Making it through another day fed and healthy was its own reward.

After my parents were both transferred to jobs in Shanghai, and I transitioned from the village to the city, I grappled with the pace and excesses of city life. The people, buses, and bicycles never stopped moving, and though there were so many more people than in my tiny village, I was lonelier than I'd ever been.

As I shared in chapter one, going to school in Shanghai was incredibly difficult for me. My teachers were right that I was not a great student, but I was not dumb. I was highly intelligent and a great learner. So I held fast to my mother's wisdom: "If you don't like something, change it."

Refusing to accept the label of "dumb," and with strong math scores which could easily contradict that perception, I channeled the grit within me to focus on a new goal: outperforming my peers in *every* subject. Conventional instruction was not teaching me language in a way that I was able to learn, so I figured out what worked for me and threw myself into it.

All the time, effort, and scarce resources I had went toward achieving this goal. Following the example of my inventive mother and my hardworking father, I wholly devoted myself to the study, practice, and pursuit of excellence.

Dyslexia, a considerable obstacle to traditional educational methods, unlocked hidden abilities for me. People with dyslexia naturally see the world differently than others. As Malcolm Gladwell says in *David and Goliath*, "Dyslexia—in best cases—forces you to develop skills that otherwise have lain dormant."[7] And so it was for me. Just as I had as a young child, I used my intellect and the resources around me—my grit—to get what I needed.

I leveraged my auditory and memory skills to develop nontraditional methods of learning English that worked for me, because in my first week of high school, I miserably failed my English exam. The late 1980s in China was still very much closed to the international community, and there weren't many materials I could get my hands on to learn English, but I scoured the shops and scraped money together until I was able to purchase a cassette player and a few English cassette tapes that I listened to over and over and over again—until the cassette player literally broke. Between that, getting any English reading material in the library, and listening to the BBC radio broadcasts at every opportunity, my strengths helped me overcome my weaknesses. A couple of years later, my efforts paid off. I achieved remarkable success in an English competition against high schoolers in Shanghai, earning three city-level awards.

This achievement attracted the attention of Fudan University, which offered me a coveted early admission to their English department and waived the requirement that I take an entrance exam. Though I hesitated initially, I used this chance as an opportunity to explore new territories and strengthen my bamboo sprout that had just begun growing.

An Expanding World

At Fudan, my commitment to English and American literature studies enabled me to win a prestigious JAL Scholarship and the rare opportunity in the early nineties to travel to Japan for a cross-cultural educational program with forty students from across the Asia-Pacific region.

Boarding my first airplane, soaring over the sea in the luxury of business class, and venturing to Japan was nothing short of life-changing. Japan was simultaneously ancient and modern. The past and the future ran parallel to each other in the towns and cities we visited.

It was as if I had stepped out of a black-and-white world and into a technicolor one. In Japan, I was like Alice in Wonderland. That experience opened up new horizons in my world.

The experience served as a catalyst for my growth, enhancing my self-confidence, enriching my worldview, and profoundly informing the trajectory of my future. As I engaged in eye-opening conversations and built relationships with my fellow students, I began to glimpse the vast array of experiences and opportunities available beyond China's borders, and I learned more about myself and what I wanted. Though I loved my homeland deeply, I felt a growing curiosity and ambition for a future that I was uncertain I could find there.

During this same time, China's historical and cultural landscape was undergoing a transformation, opening up to the international business arena. Major global corporations were entering the Chinese market for the first time, bringing cultural changes and opportunities with them.

Recognizing the golden key I possessed as an accidental English major, while I was still a college student, I took freelance jobs as an English interpreter for foreign delegations in China. I worked as a personal interpreter for the deputy prime minister of Britain and with successful business people like Richard Branson and Scott McLean.

Though international business was initially unfamiliar territory to me, I loved learning about it and immediately fell in love with it, treating each translation I provided as an opportunity to learn more.

However, it didn't take long for me to learn there was a significant pay inequality between Chinese and British employees within the company. At the time, my parents each worked jobs that paid them $100 a month. Though I was earning a healthy $300 a month as a management consultant after graduation, I found out that my British counterparts received salaries ten to twenty times that amount.

The stark difference in earnings prompted crucial questions:

Should I continue working there, driven by my passion for the field but with limited financial prospects? I could just get another job somewhere else, but I wasn't convinced that was enough of a pivot for the life I wanted.

I had to think differently.

What if I used this barrier as the starting point for exploring different dreams with greater potential for success? But where was I to go, and what was I supposed to do? The only other place I'd ever visited was Japan, and I lacked the language skills to live there on my own.

But I knew English.

So I set my sights on the United States and began to imagine my own "American dream."

Creating an Opportunity

I didn't possess much money for a big move to America, but recalling the resourcefulness of my mother and our "color" TV set, I got unconventional and resourceful. Through extensive research, I stumbled upon a few scholarship opportunities for Chinese students aspiring to study in America.

This opportunity was only just beginning to open up for Chinese students, so instead of trying to find work in America, I embraced the opportunity to keep learning about business. I took the chance and applied for a scholarship to the University of Maryland. This granted me the means to pursue an MBA, and I began to make my American dream a reality.

Like any concerned parent, my father was worried about his only child setting off to America seven thousand miles away with just a one-way ticket, two pieces of luggage, and a hundred dollars in her pocket. He tried to persuade me not to go.

I was scared too, but I leaned into the challenge, determined to surpass the barriers that were before me in China. The mental strength, courage, and tenacity I needed to take that step can directly be attributed to the people and culture that had raised me. The hard work and grit I'd learned in China are what allowed me to grow in America. The journey ahead was uncertain, but my bamboo shoot was growing stronger and taller every day.

I needed to give it room to grow, whatever the challenges that lay ahead.

New Plant, New Life, New Growth

If someone had told me that twenty-five years after I stepped onto the plane to America I would have one of the most exciting assignments in business—leveraging advanced technologies such as robotics and artificial intelligence to transform operations for FedEx, a global transportation and logistics powerhouse on the Fortune 50 list—I probably would have stared at them in disbelief, the idea too far-fetched and unimaginable for me.

I was unquestionably an underdog when I arrived in America. But my determination to fight for what I wanted was still as strong as it had been on the day my mother first sat me down for our life-changing conversation, so I did everything I could to assimilate.

I had no knowledge of popular culture or sports, and I did not drink alcohol or go to bars. Without these natural opportunities for relationships and networking, I was very alone. But I did not let that intimidate me. I leaned into the Chinese way of sharing meals with others to invite people to spend time together, to talk, and to build my own network.

Learning and thinking in English all day was exhausting. Throughout my education in China, I had been an engaged, inquisitive student raising my hand to ask questions and get to the "why" behind topics and ideas. This typically did not go over well with my teachers, as in that culture, students are expected to sit quietly and just receive the information the teacher presents. In America, the inquisitive, "disruptive" student I had once been was silenced as I had to first, translate everything being said by my professors and classmates into Chinese and then, translate my thoughts into what I wanted to say in English.

Moreover, the material I was studying was completely new to me. I was an English major with no formal business education studying for an MBA. Also, for some people, a heavy foreign accent mistakenly indicates low intelligence. Though I understood what was happening, my language skills limited my interaction with the material and people.

The turning point came when I secured a summer internship at FedEx, where my love for business and global operations blossomed and when my bamboo really took off to new heights!

After my internship, I was hired full-time as a senior marketing analyst. Though it was a promising start for me, my ambitions reached higher when I noticed there was an Asian female director in the company. I shared with my husband my newfound aspirations to become a director for the company one day, despite the challenges and time commitment it would require.

To pave the way for my dreams, obtaining a green card was the first step, a nearly five-year process that came with job restrictions. During this time, I got married and became a mother to my two daughters. Prioritizing family over career was important to me, and I was committed to first being the best mother and second nurturing my professional growth.

Though I was hungry to learn and move around many different positions in the company, once I'd learned a department and job, I got bored and was ready for the next challenge. But while my function in the company would change, it was always a lateral move, never upward. I worked hard, put in extra hours, and had high integrity, but I was not experiencing the career advancement I wanted. Despite my diligence and eagerness, I began to notice that those who started at FedEx around the time I did were being promoted over me.

Before I knew it, I had been with FedEx for eleven years. While the longevity was a testament of my dedication, my lack of upward mobility became increasingly frustrating.

Growing Deeper

Over the years, I took on a variety of positions and roles at FedEx, following my passion for learning and innovation and not the conventional corporate ladder. I pursued impact-driven job opportunities, not position-driven ones.

But as my daughters grew older and became more self-sufficient, I knew it was time to refocus on advancing my career. It was as if I had planted a brand-new bamboo seed, and I eagerly awaited the moment my bamboo shoot would break through the soil to begin its growth journey.

The fact is, though, the pace of growth is oftentimes beyond our control. I had to remain patient.

Despite years of preparation for a higher role, I was extremely disheartened when a management position opened up and I was entirely overlooked as a candidate. It devastated me. It seemed like my new bamboo seed was never going to break through the surface.

> *My life story had never been defined by stagnation; I leveraged each setback to propel myself higher.*

After a six-month period of frustration and depression, I had a pivotal conversation with my older daughter that served as a wake-up call to me when I started to take out my frustrations on my family. She didn't know what was going on at work, but she simply commented that they didn't do anything wrong. Her words reminded me that I was an overcomer (and that our family didn't deserve to be the target of my frustration). This incident encouraged me to gather my emotions, redirect my energy toward something positive, and transform the outcome instead of wallowing in self-pity.

My life story had never been defined by stagnation; I leveraged each setback to propel myself higher. Drawing from my cultural background, I embraced a Chinese perspective on crisis. In the Chinese language, the symbol for the word *crisis* combines the characters for the words *danger* and *opportunity*. This concept shifted my focus toward recognizing the opportunities amid adversity.

During this time, my understanding of management underwent a significant transformation. Initially motivated by pride, I realized from my director's wise, thoughtful guidance that true management was not about personal accolades. It was about bringing out the best in others. This revelation shifted my motivation from self-centered pursuits to a people-centric focus, which has guided my approach ever since.

I was also fortunate to have exceptional mentors and supportive individuals around me guiding me on my professional journey. Their recognition of my potential, trust in my ability to handle challenging assignments, and unwavering confidence in my abilities were instrumental in my personal growth.

I can see now that all this growth happening personally and professionally, though largely unseen, was putting down the deep roots I needed to develop in order to support tremendous future growth.

Finally, in 2010, it was as if that farmer suddenly poured Miracle-Gro on my stalled bamboo. My career soared to new heights as I became a manager leading a team for the first time, followed by a promotion to director five months later. In less than five years, I reached the position of vice president and eventually a corporate vice president.

Today I proudly serve on the board of directors for two public companies, the fruit of the deep roots I developed personally and professionally over the years.

Breaking the Bamboo Ceiling

The concept of "breaking through the glass ceiling" is akin to another lesser-known phrase in the Asian community which is "breaking the bamboo ceiling." This concept highlights the reality of barriers that prevent the advancement of Asian men and women in the workplace. Asians are often pigeonholed into certain roles or are not considered for top-tier positions due to cultural biases, stereotypes, or lack of visibility.

By overcoming these obstacles, individuals not only achieve personal success and professional growth but also contribute to broader societal change by challenging and dismantling the biases and obstacles that limit their representation in leadership positions.

During a recent conversation with my executive coach, she asked me what she thought to be a pretty general question.

She said, "Rebecca, as a female in the United States, there are certain societal expectations on the kind of role you can or should play. And when you are a woman in corporate America, there are other rules and expectations. So tell me, how did you break through those rules?"

I was genuinely confused, so I answered her question with another question, "What rules?"

She was so amused by my answer that it took her a few minutes to stop laughing. And then it hit her: I had not even recognized there were limitations to what I could or should try to accomplish in my life.

No matter your current situation, position, or level in your professional life, ignoring the unspoken rules and thinking differently about yourself, your success, and your future will unlock hidden potential and stalled success.

No matter your current situation, position, or level in your professional life, ignoring the unspoken rules and thinking differently about yourself, your success, and your future will unlock hidden potential and stalled success.

It is this spirit of unorthodox thinking that will guide you on a journey to dismantle the barriers you face, get you unstuck from where you are, and forge bold new paths in your career.

In the coming chapters, you will be challenged to embrace the unknown, invert the status quo, and discover the transformative impact of thinking differently. Together, we will embark on an extraordinary mindset shift that will reshape the course of your career and your life.

CHAPTER FOUR

THINK DIFFERENTLY

Growing up, Richard Branson had an unwelcome constant companion—dyslexia. In a traditional school setting, this learning difficulty is more than just an inconvenience; it's a significant obstacle on the path of education. Struggling with reading and writing, Branson faced not only academic challenges but also an environment that was not yet attuned to recognize and accommodate his condition.

But within the confines of this challenge lay an opportunity for a shift in perspective. Rather than becoming confined by the limits of his dyslexia, Branson leaned into his unique way of thinking. He reframed his learning difficulty as a distinctive vantage point that allowed him to see and think about things differently. He often says, "Any idea can be a great idea if you think differently, dream big, and commit to seeing it realized."[8]

Branson's distinctive style of thinking helped him to develop unique, creative strategies that others in the business world overlooked. His knack for innovation and problem-solving became the cornerstone of his ventures, enabling him to build a conglomerate of businesses that span sectors from music to space travel, collectively known as the Virgin Group.

Take, for example, his approach to launching Virgin Atlantic. Most people would be deterred by the prospect of challenging established airlines, but Branson, with his divergent thinking, saw an opportunity to disrupt the industry with superior customer service and innovative practices.

Branson's dyslexia also helped him develop an instinctive understanding of what makes a brand appealing and relatable. His ability to engage directly with consumers through his flamboyant and eccentric personality has helped Virgin's brand identity stand out in an often impersonal corporate landscape.

Richard Branson's journey from a struggling student with dyslexia to a globally renowned entrepreneur is a testament to the power of thinking differently. His story teaches us that so-called "limitations" can sometimes be the source of our greatest strengths, and it is this narrative of unconventional success that makes Branson's story captivating.

The ability to view problems and situations from unconventional angles has empowered me to explore, innovate, and question traditional methods and conventional solutions.

THNIXING DIFFREVTLY

Dyslexia causes me to see letters backward, upside down, and sometimes both (much like the heading above). Words on the page may appear jumbled together, out of order, or as if they are jumping around. The input comes into my brain, but my brain reinterprets it differently than most people's.

Over the years I've discovered that dyslexia is not a limitation but rather a unique lens through which I perceive the world. While it certainly presents challenges in processing language, it also gives me a distinct perspective that has proven to be a valuable asset in my personal and professional journey.

Much like the artistic genius of Pablo Picasso, the brilliant mind of Nikola Tesla, or the business acumen of Charles Schwab—who all had dyslexia—the condition rooted in me a way of thinking that is different from the norm. The ability to view problems and situations from unconventional angles has empowered me to explore, innovate, and question traditional methods and conventional solutions.

In high school, I was assigned to read the classic novel *Gone with the Wind*. As much as I wanted to delve into the captivating story, I knew the antiquated language would prove a significant challenge for me, and the work required for me to read it would certainly limit my enjoyment and prolong the experience.

Instead of resigning myself to defeat, I embarked on a literary journey different from my peers. I sought out the movie version of the novel and enlisted my friends to help me understand the characters and storyline. As the images danced across the screen, I was captivated by the intricate narrative and the depth of the main characters surviving the tragic history of the South during the Civil War.

By transcending the constraints of traditional reading, I was able to complete the work and enjoy the story, with the words dancing in my head instead of along the page.

Dyslexia has given me regular practice in departing from conventional methods outside the scope of language as well. It shaped my brain to habitually "think outside the box" and creatively solve problems in other areas.

In 2010, I had just been promoted to manager. Three months later, the director of the department left, and that position became open. Rather than adhering strictly to implicit conventional hiring constraints, I took a leap of faith and applied for the position.

Instead of focusing on my management track record—which, admittedly, was brief—I focused on the passion I had for the position and the cross-functional expertise I fostered during my time at FedEx. Instead of passively letting the opportunity pass by, I became energized as I showcased my unique perspectives on how to be a trailblazer in an enterprise culture change using unconventional marketing campaigns, my appetite to take educated risks, and my commitment to driving positive change (through five rounds of interviews in a two-month-long process).

By not being overly concerned with traditional timelines and expectations, I bravely opened the door to my own future.

My actions demonstrated my potential to thrive in a leadership role and proved that my impact was not limited by time but driven by my abilities and determination. As a result, I was entrusted with the director position, and from there, my career trajectory soared.

By not being overly concerned with traditional timelines and expectations, I bravely opened the door to my own future.

A Caution on Conforming

The world operates on rules and principles that provide structure and order. In nature, there are fundamental laws that govern how things function, and in every society, there are established laws that guide our behavior and interactions. Every game has rules to it, and it's the rules that make games fun and unique. Can you imagine playing *Jeopardy* without having to form the answer as a question? Without rules, you would not know what the objective to win is or how to go about reaching it. Without them, it would be anarchy and chaos. One game of checkers could last for years.

Rules are established to give structure, stability, and order. Some rules are explicit, and some are implicit. There are explicit laws for everyone in a vehicle to wear their seat belts in order to keep everyone as safe as possible. An implicit rule of driving is that when you are in a crowded parking lot, you wait patiently for a parking space and don't pull in and "steal" one from someone else who is already waiting.

Implicitly, you understand how to navigate yourself on a busy sidewalk, walking on the right and accommodating the movement of pedestrians around you to avoid collisions. Young students, however, are explicitly taught how to walk in single file through the hallways.

There are also different rules for different people. In tennis, for example, men play the best of five sets and women play the best of three. In basketball, men and women have different regulations on the size of the game ball.

Similarly, the workplace has its own set of rules, regulations, and expectations to ensure productivity, efficiency, and safety. Your company has explicit rules about work hours, but you implicitly know that if you are in a meeting or conversation with your boss at the end of the workday, you wait until its conclusion before you leave for the day. You don't just walk out the door at five o'clock (as much as you might want to).

We find comfort and security in following the rules because in doing so, we know we are inside the boundaries of what is acceptable and expected.

Psychologists call this conformity. Conformity is the tendency that both men and women have to adjust their beliefs, attitudes, and behaviors to match the norms of the groups we align with. We conform ourselves to the implicit and explicit "rules" around us.

Just think back to high school for a minute. You were explicitly told to do your homework, but no one explicitly told you who the cool kids were or what fashion trends were important to follow. You implicitly picked up on that information and either filtered it out or tried your best to conform to it.

The problem with conformity is that sometimes we are unaware of the rules we are being asked to conform to. Especially in our careers, the rules that got us here won't always get us to where we want to go (to paraphrase author Marshall Goldsmith). Nor do the rules benefit each of us equitably at each point in our careers.

Thinking differently and evaluating these rules with a fresh perspective can lead to transformative ideas and opportunities for personal and professional development.

For example, strict adherence to your supervisor's instructions is an important implicit rule to follow as you begin your career and while you are still developing your skills and reputation. But as you mature in your career, such strict adherence is no longer expected (or desired) as you gain the wisdom, insight, and experience to inform your efforts.

There is danger in becoming too reliant on conformity and adhering to the rules without critically evaluating them for yourself. As Steve Jobs once said, "Don't be trapped by dogma—which is living with the results of other people's thinking."

Discernment is crucial.

Women in particular are socialized to be "rule followers," so we don't generally mind the confines that rules offer, even when those rules hinder growth and progress. But to break free from the limitations of conforming to implicit and explicit rules and pressures we encounter, it's essential to recognize that they are there and to think differently about ones that may not serve our growth and aspirations.

Thinking differently and evaluating these rules with a fresh perspective can lead to transformative ideas and opportunities for personal and professional development. Playing by the old rules will keep you stuck and unhappy.

We cannot just blindly discard the rules, as they often serve their intended purpose. However, it is crucial to be open to questioning them and thinking differently in order to determine if they align with our individual goals and aspirations. By learning to think differently about these forces that are shaping your career, you can overcome the barriers before you and achieve success and fulfillment.

Grit Is Just the Starting Point

Like many professional women, I internalized the rule that hard work, discipline, and dedication alone would be enough to open the door to my professional success.[9] I believed grit and resilience were enough to get me to where I wanted to go and that if I "leaned in" far enough, I'd get where I wanted to be. So when I was passed over for my first management position, despite closely following these unspoken rules for so many years, I was forced to reevaluate them. If I didn't think differently about my career, I was going to hit an avoidable plateau.

> *Grit and resilience are undeniably powerful attributes, but solely relying on them isn't going to get you to your goals.*

Grit and resilience are undeniably powerful attributes, but solely relying on them isn't going to get you to your goals. Many individuals display these qualities yet find themselves stuck, unable to make significant progress in their careers. As Albert Einstein is rumored to have quipped, "Insanity is doing the same thing over and over and expecting a different result."

While grit and resilience are essential for success, there's another crucial ingredient: the ability to think differently.

Thinking differently can happen in large and small ways, and there are always benefits when it does. Thinking differently means looking beyond the boundaries and barriers that might be holding you back. It involves changing your perspective to grow in self-awareness and focus on opportunities. By embracing a fresh and original approach to the old rules, you open yourself and your future up to new solutions and pathways.

Recently, my younger daughter attended the Taylor Swift concert at Levi's Stadium in Santa Clara, California. On the day of the concert, we were made aware that the stadium only allowed clear bags to be brought in. Unable to find a suit-

When you find yourself not achieving desired results, feeling overlooked, or trapped in a state of stagnation, paralysis, or confusion, thinking differently becomes the fertilizer for your bamboo.

able bag in the shops near our hotel, she grew increasingly frustrated because she had made beaded bracelets to bring to the concert to exchange with other fans (a viral trend on the *Eras* tour).

Returning to our hotel room, she started to think differently. She took out a plastic Ziploc bag and unlaced the shoelace of a spare pair of sneakers. Poking holes at the top of the Ziploc bag, she pulled the lace through and, in under five minutes, had fashioned a working clear bag that would allow her to bring everything she needed into the stadium.

While your work and career are undoubtedly more complicated than my daughter's dilemma, the essence of getting unstuck remains similar: you must cultivate the skill of thinking differently. When you find yourself not achieving desired results, feeling overlooked, or trapped in a state of stagnation, paralysis, or confusion, thinking differently becomes the fertilizer for your bamboo. It ignites creativity and innovation, and it renews your energy and enthusiasm, empowering your career and your mind.

Reframe Your Thoughts, Reframe Your Future

I've had the pleasure of working with a mentor for over a decade, and her influence on my life has been so profound that I will credit her as the farmer in my bamboo growth journey. As an African American woman born into poverty in the South, my mentor did not allow society's "rules" around race or poverty to dictate her future. She excelled at school, fostered a love of the arts, and with grit and drive earned three postgraduate degrees from top-tier schools. Her guidance was instrumental in helping me apply thinking differently to the limiting ways I once viewed myself.

As a foreigner, I was constantly self-conscious of my accent when giving presentations at work. As I shared my insecurity in presenting before the senior leaders, my mentor was curious as to why I'd be afraid to speak.

"Oh, well, because of my accent," I said, thinking that it was as obvious and troublesome to her as it was to me.

"Everyone has an accent. There's a Boston accent, a Southern accent, all kinds of accents. You're not the only one just because you have a Chinese accent," she said.

It was as if a light bulb went off and a weight was lifted off my shoulders. I could see clearly again, and I was free to get where I needed to go.

By thinking differently, she helped me reframe my fears and put them in proper perspective. By thinking differently about the rules around you and your career, you reclaim control over your destiny and gain clarity on your direction. Thinking differently helps you define

> *Thinking differently will activate, energize, and mobilize your present and expand your future.*

what truly matters most, allowing you to make informed decisions that align with your values and aspirations.

A word of wisdom: thinking differently will activate, energize, and mobilize your present and expand your future. It unlocks possibilities you may not have envisioned before and propels you toward a more fulfilling life and dynamic career.

Opportunities Ahead

In the next section, I invite you to take an exciting journey with me as we explore some of the common rules and norms we encounter in our careers. We will develop your lens on how these expectations and pressures shape your view of yourself, your abilities, and your choices and how they constrict your potential. Together we will flip these rules on their heads to empower you to define what success looks like to you, develop your strengths, grow your network, and best of all, have a tremendous amount of fun on your way up to achieving your personal goals.

Join me as we dismantle the barriers, debunk the conventional rules, and embrace the path of innovation and growth. Let's dive in and rewrite the rules you're living by!

CHAPTER FIVE

THE GOAL RULE

While boardroom charts and meetings filled her days, it was the cadence of pounding feet and jovial laughter during twilight runs that filled Alexandra's heart and soul. She was a fixture in the local running group, and most evenings you could find her in the center of the pack, laughing with her friends as they wound their way along the pavement under the trees beneath the setting sun.

For Alex, this time allowed her to destress from her corporate job, be in nature, and meet people from her neighborhood she otherwise wouldn't have the chance to get to know.

Given her natural stride and quickness, Alex's running friends were surprised to learn that she had never run a marathon, so they encouraged her to sign up for the next one hosted in their city. Alex hadn't considered such a long-distance run before, but she took her friends' advice and registered—and then set a personal goal to cross the finish line in under four hours!

Alex dedicated herself to rigorous training for months leading up to the marathon. Evening runs in the park with friends were replaced by early morning runs in the darkness. Her lunch routine also pivoted. Instead of eating out with coworkers, she strictly followed the diet plan given by her new running coach and ate at her desk instead. Weekends were busy with long runs and sessions with her coach working on her form, speed, and endurance.

On the day of the marathon, the town was buzzing with excitement. The route was scenic, taking participants through picturesque landscapes and cheering crowds. Alex started strong, maintaining an impressive cadence. She passed the halfway mark feeling energized and focused, keeping her eye on her pace as it was being tracked by a new, expensive watch on her wrist.

As she approached the twenty-sixth mile, the final stretch of the marathon, Alex realized she was on track to achieve her goal. She crossed the finish line with a time of three hours and fifty-eight minutes, accomplishing her goal of finishing the marathon in under four hours.

Her friends and family were all gathered at the finish line, cheering at the top of their lungs, and Alex smiled in pride at her accomplishment.

A few days later however, as the initial euphoria settled, a new realization dawned on Alex: she actually felt pretty unfulfilled. You see, despite achieving her ambitious goal of completing the marathon in under four hours, there was an unexpected

You see, sometimes we achieve our goals, but we miss the mark.

sense of emptiness and even dissatisfaction. The paradox was perplexing.

For Alex, the best part of running was intertwined with the camaraderie of her friends, the relaxation of her mind, and the liberation of demands of keeping to a schedule or pace. Her friends saw her talent and meant well by encouraging her to run the marathon, but they didn't understand the underlying factors that made running so enjoyable for Alex.

The training regimen she adhered to, albeit enabling her toward her goal, put more structure than she wanted on her running. The pursuit took her completely away from her running group, siphoned her disposable income to gear and coaching, and stripped away her time with friends and coworkers. She missed the fun, freedom, stress relief, and friendship that went out the window in pursuit of her goal.

You see, sometimes we achieve our goals, but we miss the mark.

The Initial Appeal

Since 1981, when George Doran published an article in *Management Review*, the business world has been echoing the significance of setting SMART goals—ones that are specific, measurable, attainable, relevant, and time-bound. These goals are meant to be a compass, allowing us to set a course, track our progress, and adapt when setbacks arise.

We hear the often-told wisdom of Stephen Covey's book, *Seven Habits of Highly Effective People*, to "begin with the end in mind," encouraging us to reverse-engineer our path to our future goal into our actions today.

It was exactly what Alex did as she planned her marathon strategy. She meticulously charted her course, strategically laying out smaller training milestones, making adjustments, and getting help to achieve the goal.

In business, every successful company establishes annual goals and benchmarks to satisfy investors, maintain productivity, and fuel growth. Each department has goals informed by the larger goals of the company. Likewise, employees have individual goals to help them reach their full potential in their positions and maximize efficacy and efficiency.

We set personal goals for ourselves to lose ten pounds, build an emergency fund, or simply drink more water each day.

Goals offer more than just direction and focus for our choices and decisions. They carve a path before us and provide guardrails for navigating the myriad of options and distractions we face in our careers and daily lives.

If you're anything like me, there's something immensely satisfying about ticking off tasks on your to-do list, perhaps even adding completed tasks to your list for the sheer satisfaction of immediately marking them out.

How can I be certain? It's because our brains are wired for setting and reaching goals. Setting goals actually connects the heart, logic, and reward centers of the brain, which is what makes having goals so important for keeping us inspired and motivated.[10]

Studies show that when you click that checkbox on your to-do app or cross that item on your notepad, it induces your brain to release dopamine, the feel-good hormone. The ensuing surge further boosts your motivation and attention and keeps you working through the list.[11] After all, what is a to-do list but a small set of goals?

The Goal Rule

Conventional wisdom, backed by science, underscores the undeniable importance of goals, and I know this to be true in my own story. If I had not set the goal for myself to be top of my class in English, I never would have had the motivation to work as hard as I needed to achieve it. There would have been a strong temptation to live under the label of "stupid" and waste my free time on meaningless things. This academic goal was a potent catalyst that ignited my love of learning, innovation, and hard work.

In both Asian and American cultures, a typical goal for many is the attainment of a good job and financial affluence, which we are told will result in our happiness. This goal gets further broken down for us to (1) get a good education, (2) get a good job, (3) climb the corporate ladder, and (4) get money and happiness. Many Asian parents go even further to define what a "good job" looks like—with professions such as lawyer, doctor, investment banker, and engineer topping the list as good goals to have due almost exclusively to their high-income earning potential.

This goal forms an implicit rule that our lives are shaped by, and it's what I call "The Goal Rule." The Goal Rule implies we should set goals that will make us rich and happy and then do whatever we can to achieve them.

British movie actress Gemma Chan, who starred in *Crazy Rich Asians* and *Eternals*, was born in London to Chinese immigrants. A "good Chinese daughter," Gemma studied violin, piano, drama, and dance in her free time, but she understood that she was expected to get good grades so she could gain entrance to a prestigious college and find a career that would give her the money and security her parents wanted for her.[12]

Following the script her parents had given her, Gemma earned her law degree from Oxford University, but despite feeling some level of satisfaction in reaching her goal, she knew deep down that the ladder she was climbing was leaning against the wrong building.[13]

For some, like Gemma, this rule takes hold of our trajectory in the earliest days of childhood, as parents impose their goals, tirelessly strategizing and worrying over which elite preschool to secure for their child, which teams to join, or which activities to pursue. For others, it emerges later, but for nearly all of us, the pressure from this rule starts molding our thinking and decisions from high school onward. It shows up in the education we pursue, the jobs we take, the activities we allocate our free time for, and even the relationships we form. But at what cost?

Shift the Paradigm

It is certainly important to have a goal, but equally crucial is the ability to define those targets that are in sync with who you are. This becomes paramount to your happiness and success.

As Gemma pursued her law degree, it became clear to her that this was not what she wanted to do with her life. Years spent visiting the theatres of the West End with her family ignited her true passion: to be an actress. Despite the lack of Asian female representation on screen and the impending strong disapproval of her parents, Gemma finished at Oxford and enrolled in drama school to study acting.[14]

> *It is certainly important to have a goal, but equally crucial is the ability to define those targets that are in sync with who you are.*

Her parents were decidedly less than thrilled with her decision, fearing the inevitable hardship, financial struggle, and other challenges Gemma would face in the acting industry. But Gemma had made a goal for herself that aligned with who she knew she was, not who others wanted her to be. It was this agency and authenticity that propelled her forward, even as opportunities for her were scarce at first. Grit and determination carried her for over a decade in the industry until she got her breakout role in the movie *Crazy Rich Asians* in 2018.

Early on, I came to recognize that my goals needed to reflect my own priorities. When they did, I would be happiest. Perhaps it is the Confucianism and Taoism philosophies I grew up with, which both place high importance on self-discovery and personal growth, that helped me to think differently about my goals.

As a young student, I realized that the pursuit of academic excellence needed to stem from inside me. It could not be imposed by my teachers or my parents. Goals that do not align with our true selves seldom result in our happiness.

During my first eight years at FedEx, I embarked on a quest to uncover my areas of genuine interest, not simply adhering to what my education equipped me to do or the highest-paying jobs. I stayed curious about and open to various options within my career.

I still remember, two years into the marketing job, I was offered a highly coveted marketing principal position with a huge pay raise if I stayed within the analytics function. It was tempting to accept the promotion and high pay, but I wasn't sure I had enough interest to stay on. My priority was the quest to find my true passion. I stunned almost everyone when I turned down the offer and instead made a lateral move to a job in e-commerce marketing because I wanted to learn a completely new field.

My position continued to change over the next several years, but only laterally, as I learned the entire spectrum of marketing domains, from analytics, to promotions, to product development, to strategy. It literally took five extra years for me to get the same principal-level position due to the green card process. Did I regret my earlier decision? Not really. While the pay increase was a good goal that aligned with societal standards, that wasn't who I am and what was important to me. I wanted to explore during my earlier career and learn my interests and strengths, like bamboo growing deep roots. This solid foundation was what enabled me to propel my career to new heights later on.

Don't make a position, title, or bank account balance your goal; make having clarity of understanding yourself and what fills you with joy your ultimate goal.

To set the most effective and meaningful goals, you have to think differently. Don't make a position, title, or bank account balance your goal; make having clarity of understanding yourself and what fills you with joy your ultimate goal.

Beyond Expectations

When we align with our true, whole selves, and not just our goals, an astonishing truth unfolds: we can attain a level of happiness and success that exceeds even our wildest expectations.

In the span of my first decade at FedEx, I realized I did not want to proceed up the corporate ladder in marketing just for the sake of doing so. I understood the technology infrastructure of the corporation, but I also knew I did not want to be in IT. Operations, too, was within my grasp but didn't ignite my sense of purpose. My curiosity was leading me to learn about many diverse areas instead of restricting myself to one specific function or trajectory.

My reluctance to claim a goal for myself that was inauthentic ushered in a period of what felt like stagnation, but there was much growth taking place beneath the surface.

It was during this time that I was introduced to the StrengthsFinder personality inventory tool. This illuminating tool unveiled my top strengths to me, which points to the persona of a "disrupter" and "innovator." I am passionate about driving change and solving problems with new, unconventional solutions, and these strengths weren't in alignment with my function in the company at that time.

Armed with genuine self-knowledge and data, I gained the insight needed to chart a course that wouldn't just scratch the surface of success but would truly contribute to my own happiness when I achieved it.

This knowledge allowed me the clarity about myself that I needed to spend time writing out some of the key tenets of who I was, who I wanted to be, and what I wanted to get out of life. Like Gemma, I didn't know when my breakout role would arrive, but I knew I was on the right track.

Even though I didn't know where it would lead, I knew I had to follow my heart and not let either my own fear or not fitting solidly into one function, department, or path force me into a goal that would miss the mark.

Who Are You?

Bronnie Ware is a palliative care nurse who embarked on a journey of learning what the dying people she cared for wished they had done differently in their lives. A regular response from her patients was, "I wish I had the courage to live a life true to myself, not one others expected of me."[15]

Instead of chasing a transactional goal you or others think will make you happy, make sure you first truly know who you are. Make your goal clarity about yourself. Spend time discovering your strengths, learning the things that interest you, and leaning into what is important to you. Start there, and build transformational goals around who you are.

Important things to spend time considering are the following:

1) What activities do you do that make you happiest and cause you to lose track of time?
2) Who inspires you?
3) What impact do you want to have?
4) What past jobs have you loved and why?
5) What past jobs drained your energy and why?

An acquaintance of mine, Akemi, used to produce large-scale events for organizations. Each event required months of planning, organization, and attention to small details. Akemi could tolerate all these challenges because of the real joy she experienced *during* the events.

Meeting people, managing problems as they arose, and coordinating volunteers lit her up in a way that the planning work never could. She learned that human interaction, serving, and supporting others are the things that are most important to her and what she is best at. Informed by this realization, these personalized factors shape her career goals, and she's more satisfied than ever in a new job that heavily relies on her strengths.

It is important to remember that when you follow yourself, you aren't limiting your success to what already exists. I had set my goal to be a director at FedEx because that was the highest position I'd seen an Asian woman attain in the company. But when I started to focus on myself instead, the sky became the limit.

> *It is important to remember that when you follow yourself, you aren't limiting your success to what already exists.*

You might find that you are at a crossroads, questioning whether you're chasing the wrong dream. Perhaps after reading this, you're even more certain you are. If you're experiencing that sense of being on a course that does not align with who you are, take heart—you're in a great position for the breakthrough you're after.

As we begin the next chapter, we will round out your thinking about yourself by delving into a different perspective of your strengths and weaknesses. Understanding your need to follow yourself and not your goals, coupled with newfound clarity about how to think about the assets you bring, will make your next steps even clearer.

CHAPTER SIX

THE STRENGTHS RULE

E mily was a dedicated accounting consultant who spent long hours creating and analyzing reports. She was a committed team member and conscientious worker. Among her peers, she was well liked for her sharp intellect and easygoing nature, and within her firm, she earned a well-deserved reputation for her strong attention to detail and analytical skills. She was widely respected for the exceptional work she did, maintaining financial records and ensuring compliance.

Emily joined a prestigious firm right out of graduate school and hoped to climb right up the corporate ladder. However, after three years in her role as a consultant, Emily's career seemed to stall.

Frustrated by this plateau, she turned to her manager for her insight. Emily's boss told her that while she excelled in recordkeeping and had a meticulous approach to auditing, her weak leadership presence was holding her back. Emily's laid-back demeanor came across to management as lack of confidence. Her hesitancy to assert herself and her ideas in meetings and her tendency to defer to those around her were perceived as a potential liability to leadership.

Determined to fix this weakness, Emily did all she could to learn the skills of leadership. Enrolling in leadership development programs, devouring books on the subject, and developing a stronger leadership style became her mission. She poured herself into learning about leadership, and as time passed, Emily began to assert herself in more meetings to decisively respond to problems and issues. It was awkward and uncomfortable for her, but her coworkers and executives commented on the change they saw in her.

One day, while cleaning out her file drawer, Emily pulled out her past performance reviews from her time at the firm. As she scanned the pages, she noticed that on each one, listed under "Growth Opportunities," there was a comment or two about her weaknesses. Buoyed by her recent success in developing her weak leadership skills, she made notes of the other things mentioned, such as poor presentation skills and public speaking.

Sure that now she had discovered the key that would unlock her future success, Emily feverishly worked on learning PowerPoint, watching TED Talks to uncover the secrets of top-notch presentations.

Eighteen months later, Emily received the call she'd been waiting for. There was a vacant management position in the department, and Emily's boss had just called her into his office.

In the Boss's Office

Unfortunately for Emily, the anticipated promotion was not what lay behind her boss's office door that day.

"Emily, I'd like you to meet David," he said. "He will be our new department manager."

Emily's heart sank.

David politely introduced himself, and over the next few minutes, Emily learned he'd been in the firm's London office for two years and had recently moved back. His exposure to global markets and international experience made him a prime candidate for the management position.

Despite all the progress she'd made in her leadership and communication skills over the last two years, despite her well-earned reputation and her track record of integrity, she was simply no competition for David's robust international experience.

All of a sudden, it occurred to Emily that she had been so busy fixing her weaknesses that she hadn't cultivated her strengths. While her skills had improved, she was seen (and saw herself) as someone who could perform the function but not someone with unique skills and gifts to bring to the table.

Unfortunately for us, our brains are hardwired with what psychologists call a negativity bias.

To break through, she knew she had to differentiate herself, and fixing her weaknesses wasn't going to be what did it.

Not Good Enough

There are hundreds of assessments to help professionals learn their strengths and weaknesses. Some cast a wide net, offering insights into general personality traits, while others are tailored to particular industries or occupations, pinpointing individual gifts and areas for improvement with scientific accuracy.

A certain affirmation arises when you take one of these tests and see your strengths laid out before you in black and white. It's a recognition of your talents and abilities and an affirmation of the contributions you offer. Equally enlightening is the revelation of your weaknesses and the areas where growth is needed.

Unfortunately for us, our brains are hardwired with what psychologists call a negativity bias. This means that when we are given positive and negative feedback, we naturally focus our attention more on the negative.[16]

This happens all the time in various scenarios at work: your boss applauds the report you diligently crafted but suggests a formatting tweak, and suddenly, you're mentally chastising yourself for your initial choice. A customer provides glowing feedback but casually mentions one area of minor dissatisfaction, and you find yourself ruminating on it into the wee hours.

This also happens when we take an assessment that calls out our strengths and weaknesses; we zero in on the weaknesses and downplay or even disregard our strengths. We live in a world fascinated by the need to fix our weaknesses and rectify our shortcomings. There are thousands of books, courses, and tools geared to helping a person develop their weaknesses in any and every area.

In the Asian culture, it's very common for parents to compare their children with the children of their friends and neighbors. If the other kids appear to be more successful, parents interpret this as a reflection of their child's inadequacies. The result is often undue pressure on their kids to perform in similar capacities, often ignoring their own kids' unique interests, talents, and specialties.

We all fall into the trap of comparing our weaknesses to others' strengths, whether it's around the water cooler or while scrolling social media. It's a disheartening endeavor for anyone. This obsession with shortcomings inevitably leaves us in a perpetual state of not feeling good enough and certainly not feeling empowered and invigorated. Focusing on weaknesses tends to diminish our confidence and negatively impacts our work. When we find ourselves frantically attempting to shore up our weaknesses, it can feel like we're running on a never-ending treadmill, expending twice the effort just to maintain the pace.

Lean In (To Your Strengths)

We all have many weaknesses; that is certain. However, the grand fallacy many of us mistakenly succumb to is spending our lives trying to fix those weaknesses, thinking that doing so will help us be "good enough" by our or someone else's standards. This implicit rule will undoubtedly improve our baseline, but it will probably not be enough to lead to a breakthrough.

I think that it is focusing on your strengths that will enable you to stand out and get ahead.

In your areas of weakness, your skills tend to fall below the average. If you channel your efforts to improve your weaknesses, you can indeed elevate your skills to the point where they become adequate. But when you invest the same amount of energy in amplifying your strengths, you further distinguish yourself from average and better position yourself for success.

There is an opportunity cost to focusing all your energy on fixing your weaknesses as well. With limited time in the day to devote to self-improvement, by singularly focusing on developing your weaknesses, you miss out on exciting opportunities for elevating your strengths and developing the conditions to differentiate yourself from your peers.

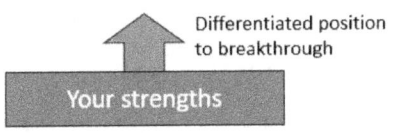

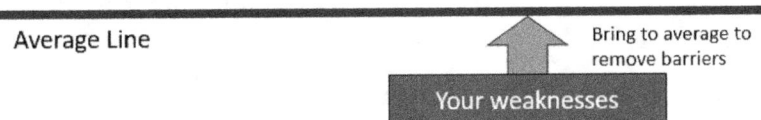

In most sports, the players need to be able to play some degree of both offense and defense. When we wholeheartedly embrace our strengths, it's like playing offense; it's what propels us forward because our strengths are what set us apart from the pack. Conversely, when our focus remains on simply improving our weaknesses, we're only playing defense, just trying to protect our current position. Women in particular often see their weaknesses as bigger barriers than men do. Oliver-Wyman reports that "a woman often won't apply to a job unless she feels she meets one-hundred percent of the described qualifications. In contrast, for men, this number is more like sixty per-cent."[17] When we refuse to progress until we've fixed all our weaknesses, we are only playing defense, and it is really hard to win any game by only playing defense!

> *When we wholeheartedly embrace our strengths, it's like playing offense; it's what propels us forward because our strengths are what set us apart from the pack.*

To be successful, you too must play both offense and defense. Developing your weak-nesses is important; it helps remove the barriers that come between you and the success you're after. But it's not the only solution. Leaning into your strengths is what catapults you to win.

Your strengths are a defining part of your identity. As you pour energy into cultivating them, you'll become en-ergized and invigorated instead of feeling like you're just playing catch-up. Your confidence grows, you become more joyful, and your work will become more fulfill-ing as well.

Researcher Tom Rath, author of *StrengthsFinder 2.0*, affirms this in his findings as well. "People have several more times more potential for growth when they invest energy in developing their strengths instead of correcting their deficiencies."[18]

Clarity through Strengths

When I was in my thirties, I struggled with my career path. Being hardworking and curious, I excelled at each assignment in the company, but I was never interested in fully committing to a department or function. I usually lost interest once I learned everything about a department and was already looking for where I could go next to learn something new. I wondered if there was something wrong with me. Why couldn't I stick to one function? What would this mean for my career?

It wasn't until 2010, when I was introduced to StrengthsFinder, now known as CliftonStrengths, that I could fully identify my strengths. The test shed great insight into me as a person and identified my top talents. The test showed me that I think in strategic and futuristic ways, that ideation comes naturally to me, and that I'm a strong learner. It showed me that I am an innovator and a disruptor who likes to "play in the white space"—solving undefined problems and embracing new challenges. It was no wonder that I got bored after a while in my various functions!

Once I understood this, it helped me manage my frustration with myself and navigate the best opportunities for myself. Within FedEx, as in any large company, each function and department has clearly defined roles and responsibilities. I cannot change the organizational structure, but I could be more intentional in focusing on roles in FedEx that allow me the freedom I need to use my strengths. Knowing my strengths allowed me to position myself at the intersection of my goals and my passions.

Over the past decade, I've flourished in the innovation and advanced technologies spaces, feeling like a fish effortlessly swimming in the open sea rather than struggling helplessly on the shore. This professional fulfillment has spilled over into a great sense of personal fulfillment and led to success and opportunities I'd never dreamed about.

"Is There Anything You Are Good At?"

Nancy and I shared a table at an Asian Pacific Islander Network (APIN) summit in 2019. She vented her frustrations, detailing how people constantly highlighted her shortcomings, implying she wasn't management material. After patiently listening to her litany of complaints, I posed a single question:

> *The significance of leaning into our strengths extends far beyond the workplace; it enriches our personal lives too.*

84

"So, is there anything you are good at?"

Her initial perplexity gave way to enthusiasm as she detailed her strengths. "Well, I am very organized. I love operations, things in motion. I like to work on the front line, and I get things done . . ."

Based on these insights, I suggested she consider a role in operations management.

It wasn't until recently that I learned just how impactful that one question was for Nancy. At a recent APIN summit, Nancy shared with the attendees the impact that one question had on her life. She had taken my words to heart and, four years later, had gone from being a team member to a senior manager in operations. What a change!

The significance of leaning into our strengths extends far beyond the workplace; it enriches our personal lives too. My passion lies in solving ambiguous and complex problems, but my husband is the opposite.

As an engineer, he thrives on well-defined problems and predictability. We respect each other for who we are. If he was trying to be like me, or I was trying to be like him, we would be miserable, and our marriage wouldn't work. These complementary strengths we each bring to our marriage are what make it strong.

Knowing your strengths does not mean you ignore your weaknesses.

Understanding the unique strengths of my children also liberates me from any "tiger mom" tendencies. Instead of being critical and controlling, I can help them develop their unique skills and strengths. This mindset allows them to blossom without the limiting pressures of the (perceived) strengths of the children around them.

Following your strengths and passions and surrounding yourself with people who do the same—that's the path to a joyful, fulfilling life!

Know Your Strengths

"Do you have an opportunity to use your strengths every day? Chances are, you don't. All too often, our natural talents go untapped. From the cradle to the cubicle, we devote more time to fixing our shortcomings than to developing our strengths," eloquently states CliftonStrengths, a venerable strengths assessment tool.[19]

Uncovering and cultivating your strengths is not hard. In fact, it's often an enjoyable journey. But first, you must identify them.

Taking a test like CliftonStrengths or reading the book *StrengthsFinder 2.0* can help identify where your strengths lie. But don't just read the results you get. Study them to understand what each strength really means, and allow the results to help you build more clarity.

Knowing your strengths does not mean you ignore your weaknesses. You just need to keep them in context and rely on your strengths to differentiate yourself. Asking for insights about your strengths and weaknesses from those who know you well can be a real gift—if you open yourself up to listen. Ask those around you what you do well and where you could grow. When presented with their perspectives, don't get defensive, don't try to prove them wrong. Just nurture curiosity and say, "Tell me more."

In leadership training, one of the first exercises we did was a "360" feedback exercise. This involved collaring anonymous feedback from people all around you (hence the 360 expression). I was shocked to receive the feedback from some of my peers that I was perceived as "verbose and trying to be the smartest person in the room."

I was so confused.

An outsider and underdog, I never considered myself to be better than others. I couldn't believe what I was hearing. But I leaned into my strengths of curiosity and learning and asked for more details. I was enlightened to learn that people thought I was verbose because I repeated my sentences and often reiterated the same idea in different ways. I reflected and realized that it was true: I did repeat myself. Because English is not my first language, I often operated under the assumption that my words and message weren't clear, so I would repeat myself a few times and in different ways. The redundancy was in an attempt at clarity but was being misconstrued as arrogance.

I could have been very offended at the feedback, closing the door on growth. By leaning into my strengths, I ended up discovering something I never would have known otherwise.

Effortless Action

Each person is unique, and what we define as success and the paths we take to get there are all different. Instead of fighting to be average, we can embrace the things that will set us apart. Embracing these strengths is the key to achieving the inner harmony and peace contained in the ancient Chinese wisdom of wu wei. Instead of striving to keep up or be enough, you can simply lean into being authentically you.

When you embrace your strengths, the action becomes almost effortless.

When you embrace your strengths, the action becomes almost effortless. Your confidence increases, and your determination, grit, and resilience root you for the success to come—just like the bamboo. You become secure in your identity and confident in your direction, aware that at any moment, your growth will take off!

As your understanding of your goals and strengths deepens, you'll find that opportunities to leverage these strengths will naturally arise before you.

In the next chapter, we will start to put your strengths to work.

CHAPTER SEVEN

THE OPPORTUNITY RULE

M iranda is a diligent software engineer at a bus-
tling tech firm. One afternoon she attended an
innovation seminar her company organized. The mood
in the auditorium was electric as industry leaders shared
their insights, and Miranda buzzed with excitement and
inspiration. She could feel her horizons broadening.

During a stretch break, she grabbed a cup of coffee
and bumped into a young woman named Jessica. Jessica
was a rising star in the tech world, and they struck up an
easy conversation. Jessica mentioned the new project she
was leading and spoke passionately about her vision.

Miranda was intrigued. Jessica's project was something that perfectly suited her own personal skills and
interests, and she would love to work with a leader as

engaging and inspiring as Jessica. They wrapped up their conversation and exchanged contact information, and before Miranda returned to her seat, Jessica told her to call her some time so they could talk again.

Over the next few weeks, Miranda would wonder about Jessica and the project, but she never reached out to Jessica about it. She would tell herself that she didn't have enough experience or that Jessica was just being nice and that Jessica's team was surely already in place for such an incredible project.

After a few months, Miranda's curiosity got the better of her, and she typed out a nervous email to Jessica. Jessica's reply was almost immediate. She told Miranda she was so happy to hear from her and had been hoping she would email months ago. They'd had a vacancy on their team and needed someone with Miranda's skills, but since Jessica never heard from Miranda, they filled the position.

As Miranda read the reply, she let out a deep sigh, painfully aware that she'd just let a great opportunity pass her by.

What's Luck Got to Do With It?

People often feel as if opportunities are elusive. It is common to believe that while working hard and developing strengths are good practices, ultimately, success is entirely dependent on luck. It's a feeling that needing to be at the right place at the right time is essential. I understand this feeling, and I do believe there is significance in timing and circumstances.

Perhaps you're excelling in your current role, but your manager appears content with the status quo, leaving you apprehensive about your own stagnation. Meanwhile, in another department, a colleague's manager departs, creating an unexpected opening for her advancement. You can't help but think, "She's so lucky."

However, this notion that opportunity is solely a matter of luck can foster passivity and even a victim mentality. Reflect on your own emotional response when you witness scenarios like I've just described in the workplace. Are you inspired to work harder and take chances? Or does it leave you frustrated, feeling as if your goals are out of reach and any success you have is a by-product of events outside your control?

Thinking differently allows you to realize that opportunity isn't an elusive force but is something within your grasp that you can actively influence. Realizing this empowers you and gives you the strength needed to drive yourself forward. This perspective allows you to take control, welcome calculated risks, and take chances, knowing that while success is never guaranteed, a well-chosen opportunity is a valuable stepping stone toward your goal . . . if you're courageous enough to take it.

There are two facets of opportunity: first, the ability to identify promising opportunities when they arise, and second, the readiness to take action when it does.

> *There are two facets of opportunity: first, the ability to identify promising opportunities when they arise, and second, the readiness to take action when it does.*

But what if you have hesitated in the face of opportunities in the past? What if hindsight has been your greatest teacher, whispering lessons and regrets about the chances you've let pass or ones you've taken that didn't pan out? What if you find yourself in a sea of regret and discouragement?

Rest assured, opportunities themselves do not lead to your desired outcomes. It's your actions that wield the power, and your actions are entirely within your control.

Opportunity is more than luck or timing. It's about recognizing the *right* opportunities for you and having the courage to take hold of them. A good opportunity may appear daunting at first because it may lie outside your routine, comfort zone, or expectations. Sometimes opportunities may take you by surprise or lead you down entirely new paths, requiring unanticipated but exciting pivots. But even if an opportunity arises and veers off course from your initial expectations, it has still bestowed on you the gift of growth and prepared you for the steps ahead. In contrast, past inaction is irreparable, casting long shadows of regret. As actress Gemma Chan aptly said, "Disappointment is a temporary thing. Regret lasts forever."

Go for It!

When a good opportunity arises, you must be prepared to take advantage of the chance you're given. There is no amount of skill, knowledge, or experience that will ever be able to guarantee your success every time. You have to do the best you can with what you have already acquired and developed in yourself, and have the courage to take a chance on yourself. After all, there is no one more invested in your success than you!

Distinguishing the right opportunities from the distracting ones becomes easier once you've honed in on your goals and strengths

Distinguishing the right opportunities from the distracting ones becomes easier once you've honed in on your goals and strengths. Often this is what gets mistaken for luck. Opportunities, when coupled with direction and preparation, often appear to others as fortuitous and effortless.

In my own life, as a young woman with dreams beyond China's horizons, I recognized the opportunity that awaited me if I took the step to pursue my graduate education in America. I recognized my capacity for quickly adapting and learning, and I leaned on those skills as I took the leap. Had I focused on my nonnative language struggles, the foreignness of life in America, or how far away from home it was, fear might have dissuaded me from the opportunity, and my entire life would have taken a very different course.

> *It's not solely these opportunities themselves that pave the way to success; it's your taking action that truly counts.*

Similarly, when I encountered a vacant director position in my department, I easily identified this as a golden opportunity and pursued it wholeheartedly. When I understood the power at the intersection of technology and business applications, again, I leaned into my strengths to accomplish my goal of influencing the corporate culture of a Fortune 50 company.

In your journey, following your passion, leaning on your strengths, and patiently pursuing these with grit and resilience will enable you to spot and embrace the right opportunities as they arise. It's not solely these opportunities themselves that pave the way to success; it's your taking action that truly counts.

Peggy Cherng may not have the same household name recognition as Oprah Winfrey or Sheryl Sandberg, but she stands atop them all as number ten on the Forbes list of the wealthiest self-made women in America as of 2023, with a net worth of $3.1 billion.[20]

Her journey as the cochair and cochief executive officer of Panda Restaurant Group, the parent company of Panda Express, exemplifies her remarkable ability to seize opportunities and achieve success that aligns with her goals.

Originally from Hong Kong, Peggy moved to the United States to pursue a college education, where she met her future husband, Andrew Cherng. After graduating with a degree in electrical engineering, Peggy embarked on her professional journey by working with 3M and McDonnell Douglas and coding simulators for the US Navy.

Following the passing of her father-in-law, the unexpected opportunity arose for Peggy to make a pivot and join her husband in running the family restaurant, Panda Inn. The popularity of their restaurant opened the door for the opportunity to start a quick-serve version of their popular restaurant in the local mall, giving birth to Panda Express.

As their restaurant's popularity soared, and her husband worked to expand to other locations, Peggy saw a different opportunity. Always the engineer, she took it upon herself to streamline operations and introduced innovative practices to enhance efficiency and customer satisfaction.

Her introduction of the "point-of-sale" system, a ground-breaking concept at the time, revolutionized order processing. She took chances by taking advantage of the opportunities that came her way that aligned with her gifts, goals, and visions for the company and didn't let those opportunities pass her by.[21]

> *You are most effective and happiest at the intersection of your passions, strengths, and opportunities.*

Not All Opportunities Are Equal

You are most effective and happiest at the intersection of your passions, strengths, and opportunities. This juncture is the ultimate sweet spot. In the corporate world, I've witnessed many individuals equate opportunity with promotion, chasing titles, and salary hikes rather than aligning opportunities with their goals and strengths.

True happiness resides in people who put themselves in positions that intersect with their goals, passions, and priorities, regardless of the job title. You can maximize your capabilities, achieve breakthroughs, and still be aligned with your goals and values.

Lining up your journey and passions with the right opportunities requires resilience and grit. It necessitates a steadfast focus on your growth and goals without succumbing to the discouragement or distraction of transient temptations. During this waiting period, each of us is presented with another opportunity: to prepare ourselves for our desired future.

In my own journey, mentors and executive coaches were indispensable in helping me navigate moments of frustration, confusion, and self-doubt, facilitating my growth as I waited for the right opportunities.

This period resembles the unseen growth of the bamboo, where you establish deep roots, acquire knowledge and wisdom, and gain clarity on your goals and strengths. As you wait, resist the temptation to rely on luck or take the conventional path.

> *Discerning opportunities warrants a profound understanding of oneself, a commitment to personal growth, and the courage to make choices that align with your priorities.*

In my first five years as vice president, several executive vice presidents invited me to assume lateral positions in functional areas they oversaw. Their rationale was that doing so would increase my chances of being promoted to a senior executive position, and it undoubtedly would have. However, that wasn't my ambition. I am driven by my passion for innovation in advanced technologies space, not positions, so I made the deliberate choice to wait and grow, trusting the right opportunity would come along.

Similarly, Peggy and Andrew Cherng had the opportunity to take their company public and make even more money from the deal. However, they recognized going public would require them to shift their leadership approach to prioritizing profits over people, a shift that was incongruent with their values. So they let the opportunity go and remained resolute in charting a way forward that was authentic to who they were and the company they wanted to build.

Discerning opportunities warrants a profound understanding of oneself, a commitment to personal growth, and the courage to make choices that align with your priorities.

Don't Give Up!

If you aspire to take control of your future and break free from stagnation, taking advantage of the opportunities that come your way is not the only way to reach your goals. You possess the ability to create for yourself the opportunities you need to move forward. Initiating such opportunities begins with cultivating a clear understanding of your desires, honing your strengths, and nurturing your skill set and your network.

Don't hesitate to share your quest for opportunities with the people you know. A friend of mine, a marketing analyst at a medical device company, loves photos. In her spare time, she started to learn about professional photography and took the courage to grow a side business on the side. Initially, there was very little business and fees she could charge, but her unique appreciation of human interactions, facial expressions, angles of scenery and lighting made her photos stand out. Word of mouth helped her grow a reputation as a successful wedding and family photographer, and now her side business exceeds her day job. The most rewarding feeling for her goes beyond money: it is living her passion to capture beautiful moments of life. If avenues to your desired opportunities remain elusive, consider going back to your drawing board to define your passion first.

Slow Down to Speed Up

Depending on luck is not enough to break free of inertia. Inaction spawns regret and stagnation, and acting on opportunities simply for the sake of action often culminates in distraction and future frustrations. So what should you do?

To truly harness the right opportunities, you must first cultivate clarity.

To truly harness the right opportunities, you must first cultivate clarity. Creating a "clarity touchstone" (see chapter eleven), where you delineate your passions, strengths, and goals, will serve as a compass guiding your journey and discerning what opportunities you have, and which ones you need to create.

When you dare to embrace the risks presented in a good opportunity, you may expose yourself to failure. However, remember that even failure is an opportunity. In chapter eight, we will dig deeper into how failure can unexpectedly become the driving force that propels your career forward.

CHAPTER EIGHT

THE LIMITS RULE

The vast fields of Southern California, with their swaying crops and sun-baked soil, were José Moreno Hernández's earliest playgrounds. Born into a migrant family who followed the seasonal harvests, his days were spent either in helping in the fields or, when he could be spared, in a local school's classroom.

Because the initial years of José's life were spent constantly on the move, his education was inconsistent at best. But he was a determined learner and a gifted mathematics student, so he was able to get by. A turning point came one year in the form of a simple, poignant question posed by one of his second-grade teachers to José's father.

"If you plant a fruit tree, water it, and then uproot it to plant it elsewhere again and again, what do you think will happen to the tree?" The profound meta-phor was not lost on his father, who understood that, like a tree, his children needed roots to truly thrive and blossom. This realization led to a life-altering decision: the family gave up the transient life of migrant farmers and settled in one place, allowing José a stable environ-ment to pursue his education.

About this time, José watched *Apollo 11*'s journey to the moon, and it inspired a dream: he wanted to become an astronaut. From that day forward, it became his one and only goal, and he did everything he knew to do to become educated enough for such a career.

After graduating from the University of California, Santa Barbara, with a master's degree in electrical and computer engineering, José's relentless pursuit of this goal led him to an entry-level engineering position at the Lawrence Livermore National Laboratory. He worked on advanced space propulsion systems, which not only honed his skills but brought him one step closer to his dream. He began applying to NASA's training program.

With his first application, he was met with his first rejection. For many, such a rejection from an institution as prestigious as NASA might have been the end of the road. But for José, it was merely a detour. He understood that dreams as big as the universe required sacrifices, re-silience, and an unwavering spirit.

Instead of wallowing in disappointment, or just giving up altogether, José set out to better himself. He took up a rigorous physical training regimen, understanding the demands of space on the human body. He became a licensed pilot. He took lessons and was scuba certified. Each of these endeavors wasn't just a hobby; they were stepping stones, meticulously planned and executed, to bring him closer to space.

He applied again and again, year after year. He was rejected every single time, until his twelfth application. In 2004, rather than receiving a response letter from NASA beginning with the familiar, "We are sorry to inform you . . . ," it began with, "Congratulations!"

José Moreno Hernández traveled to space as the mission specialist aboard the shuttle *Discovery* for fourteen days in August of 2009.

Know Your Limits

A limitation, by definition, is a constraint on what is deemed permissible or possible. Each individual invariably encounters limitations as an inherent facet of life. Moreover, every system and organization we are involved in puts limits around us, some fairly and some unfairly. Fair limitations manifest themselves in different forms like budgets, timelines, roles, and responsibilities, all meticulously crafted to not only reduce haphazard pursuits but to guide our actions with proficiency and efficiency.

My assistant, Lesa, and I both understand the limits that define our positions at FedEx. I don't assume her responsibilities, and she does not assume mine. The limits of our roles dictate the tasks and parts we play in the organization.

Nevertheless, to pursue a professional breakthrough means to surpass the perceived capabilities, expectations, and limits you've operated under. When you are stuck and looking for a breakthrough, knowing your limits is the starting point, but not the end.

Conventional wisdom suggests that you must know your limits so you can stay within them. I say, be aware of your *current* limits, but look for ways to surpass them.

You must think differently about your limits so you can push past them, but the fact is that right outside your limits lies the chance of failure. "Feeling like a failure" does not connote a positive, hopeful emotion. It evokes disappointment, discouragement, and even shame. Staying within our limits seems to offer us the chance to avoid such negative emotions and experiences while offering us moderate levels of what feels like guaranteed success.

If you always stay within your limits, you minimize your risks of failure, but you also minimize your chances of growth.

To grow, you must be willing to learn. To learn, you must be willing to try. And to try, you must be willing to fail. Failure is scary, unknown, and unfortunately, often vilified. But failure is not necessarily a bad thing. If you never fail, you won't ever succeed in fulfilling your potential.

> *Failing is just an opportunity to pivot and try something new to overcome your limits and get closer to your goal.*

In the early stages of my career, I received feedback that said, "Rebecca doesn't know her limitations." It wasn't delivered with malice, nor did I perceive it as a criticism. It was true. The concept of limitations has never meant barriers to me. Either because of nature or nurture, I see limitations only as obstacles and not dead ends.

Failing my high school English exam in the first week of school made me feel as if the whole world could see that I had reached my limit. But here's an essential insight I learned in that experience: limits are not fixed. They will grow and stretch with you as you push against them and wrestle them down so you can transcend them. Failing is just an opportunity to pivot and try something new to overcome your limits and get closer to your goal.

In response to having reached my limit, but not my potential, I committed myself to expanding my skills and

107

knowledge to further and further push my limits, until I surpassed my peers' performance and everyone else's expectations.

While some may see failure lurking on the other side of our limits, I want to warn you that simply staying within them won't render you impervious to it. In fact, staying within your limits could lead to the failure to achieve the very goals and aspirations you hold dear.

Push Past Your Limits

When a baby is learning to walk, she gradually pushes the limits of what she can do, developing incremental skills needed in the process.

First, she pulls herself up from crawling on all fours to standing with support. When that skill is proficient, she starts standing without support. Then, she gets really brave and starts moving her feet away from the security of the furniture or hands she is holding, and she starts trying to walk unassisted. Her first step is shaky, but as she persists, she gets stronger and can walk with balance and ease.

At each point in her development, the baby learning to walk will fall repeatedly. No person has ever learned to walk without falling! Yet when a baby is learning to walk, the goal of each attempt is not to walk a predetermined number of steps but to push her limits a little further until she is developmentally ready to take off.

Like a butterfly leaving its cocoon, you must push and pull against your limits to break free. To transcend your limitations, you must be willing to embrace new challenges and understand that

Failure is really just an invitation to pivot, a chance to push your boundaries in different directions toward improved outcomes.

initial success is rare. You might stumble. You could fall. But when you see failure as an end point, you're only seeing a fraction of the picture.

By adopting a growth mindset, you can reframe your perspective and instead begin to see more clearly that failure is really just an invitation to pivot, a chance to push your boundaries in different directions toward improved outcomes. A growth mindset will help you see that to reach your potential, you need to aim past any fixed targets and strive for the continuous expansion of your limits.

There's a saying often attributed to Steve Jobs that says, "A students work for B students, and B students work at companies started by C students." This isn't an encouragement to laziness or mediocrity, but it's a recognition that it is by the absence of success (failure) that we learn the skills of grit, resilience, innovation, and determination. We also become a little less afraid of failing, having stared it in the face.

There's nothing wrong with being an A student, but A students sometimes only learn to replicate their results by repeating past actions for fear of failure. B and C students have to work to improve their grades and learn new skills, new strategies, and new techniques to achieve success, and the end result becomes a wider breadth of knowledge, experience, and possibilities.

It was certainly true for me.

If you want to grow, you must know your limits and then take risks and chances that push you past them. Might you fail? Certainly. But as J. K. Rowling says, "It is impossible to live without failing at something, unless you live so cautiously that you might as well not have lived at all—in which case, you fail by default."[22]

Fail Wisely

Failure serves as a customized opportunity to gain knowledge tailored to you and your unique situation. Armed with this new knowledge, you can make adjustments and try again to overcome your limits. As Thomas Edison said concerning his failures along the way in his process of inventing the light bulb, "I have not failed. I've just found 10,000 ways that don't work."[23]

To step out of your comfort zone and risk failure is to open yourself to unprecedented opportunities. In doing so, you not only expand your own boundaries but also those of the people around you. Take, for example, the remarkable story of Simone Biles, the most decorated US gymnast. At the age of twenty-four, after an eighteen-month hiatus from competition, Simone exploded back on the gymnastics stage at the US Classic in 2021.

Her routine featured a Yurchenko double pike vault, an extraordinarily challenging maneuver. This limit-pushing move demands not only considerable strength and precision but also unwavering mental fortitude due to its inherent danger. A misstep during the final flip could result in a severe head or neck injury.

Until 2021, this feat had only been accomplished by male gymnasts, with no woman even daring to attempt it in competition. However, Simone possessed the courage to stretch her limits, to transcend established norms, ultimately expanding the horizons for all female gymnasts.[24]

Undoubtedly pushing boundaries and embracing the prospect of failure requires embracing discomfort. However, this doesn't equate to embracing recklessness. It's crucial to assess risks thoughtfully, weighing the costs of failure against the opportunities. Not all failures are created equal. Simone, for instance, rigorously trained and implemented safety measures before attempting the vault. If she hadn't, she would have jeopardized her Olympic prospects, her physical well-being, and even her life.

Distinguishing between pushing a limit and making a foolish mistake is imperative. There's a chasm between calculated risk and reckless risk. Rushing through due diligence for the sake of taking risks is ill-advised. Be deliberate and intentional about the limits you seek to surpass and how and when you pursue growth.

In my field, technology and innovation, risk is inherent. However, it's a manageable element when you comprehend market trends, technological shifts, customer demands, and the readiness of business initiatives. With this knowledge, I can take calculated risks, avoiding the randomness of dart-throwing tactics. Doing so helps me to expand my limits on knowledge and experience.

It's important to acknowledge that not everyone shares the same comfort level with taking risks. Personal dispositions and experiences play a significant role. Listening to your instincts can be valuable, particularly when the path forward is unclear, as your emotional responses are rooted in your unique life experiences.

Fail Small

Not all risks yield equal benefits, and it's worth noting that failure isn't always a pleasant teacher. In some situations, failure might have serious repercussions, even potentially costing you your job. If you find yourself in an environment where failure is not tolerated, where innovation is discouraged, and the status quo reigns supreme, my advice is straightforward: consider other options. Remaining in such a stifling atmosphere is a form of entrapment. If you can't fail, you can't grow.

You're in "permanent beta," and your goal is to continually be experimenting, learning, and evolving.

When others curtail your opportunities, they simultaneously cap your potential for success.

In the book *The Startup of You*, Reid Hoffman, cofounder and chairman of LinkedIn, introduces the concept of being in "permanent beta." When a product or software is in beta mode, it undergoes real-world testing to ensure its functionality. This testing reveals flaws and weaknesses, allowing for refinement and, ultimately, success in the market.

Similarly, if we view ourselves as being in "permanent beta," we accept that we are continually tested, always a work in progress, constantly pushing our boundaries, and perpetually discovering ways to improve.

Success demands that we all push our limits. Experiment with new approaches, and accept the possibility of failure. Embrace the discomfort that these opportunities and the fear of failure may stir within you. Expand your limits, and be receptive to the success that awaits beyond them.

If you want to get unstuck, you have to try new things, get out of your comfort zone, take risks, fail, and try again. Living within your limits because you're afraid to fail will only constrain your growth. Remember, you're in "permanent beta," and your goal is to continually be experimenting, learning, and evolving. This perspective can alleviate some of the pressure, reminding you that you're simply exploring new possibilities, assessing how you respond to challenges, and ultimately discovering your path forward.

Understanding your limitations is certainly valuable, but it should never serve as an excuse for complacency. Recall the example of a baby learning to walk. It's a gradual process of increasing skill and capacity as limits expand from crawling to walking and then running. The baby does not quit because she was unable to run a marathon on her first attempt.

Similarly, with a goal to broaden your limits, you must take baby steps to get there.

If you fear public speaking, start by setting the goal to speak up in at least three meetings a month. Don't sign up to deliver a TED Talk next week. If you want a leadership role but lack confidence, volunteer for small roles within your team or community. If you're uncomfortable with networking, start with smaller events or gatherings and make it your goal to build one meaningful connection at each event.

Incrementally challenge your limits, and gradually escalate your efforts. These small steps allow room for learning, pivoting, and adjusting before tackling more significant risks. Along the way, you build skills and increase your comfort level.

Root for Yourself

Life is an intricate journey filled with twists, turns, peaks, and valleys. This very unpredictability is what makes it truly exciting. The highs and lows offer opportunities for learning and growth, and failure is an inevitable part of this process. Once you embrace the fact that failure can never be entirely avoided, you can accept it, learn from it, and pivot toward becoming a better, more successful individual in the future.

Should you find the concept of living beyond your limits daunting, exercise patience with yourself during the process. In psychology, there's a concept known as deconditioning, which suggests that systematic exposure to something you fear can help you overcome that fear.

So dare to fail in small, manageable ways, and do so persistently. Over time you'll discover that it becomes easier to face challenges and grow.

Think of each attempt you make to leave your comfort zone and push your limits as akin to a tiny new root put out by the bamboo slowly growing and anchoring itself for future growth.

In our next chapter, we'll move beyond the limiting rule that you must choose between a successful career and a fulfilling life. We'll help you craft a vision for a life where you fulfill your potential while maintaining the balance you desire.

CHAPTER NINE

THE EITHER-OR RULE

From when she was a child, Jennifer cherished the trips she took with her parents to the tranquil mountains. The days of exploring in the woods and time spent by the mountain streams watching the bugs and birds were etched in her memory. As a grown woman with a young family of her own, she had been excited to introduce her kids to the peace and fresh mountain air she held so dear. A photograph from their recent mountain vacation occupied a special place on Jennifer's desk, nestled amid the stacks of file folders and business reports. As she gazed at the picture, her heart swelled with fond memories. Yet if she was being honest, mingled with that warmth was an undercurrent of anxiety.

At work, Jennifer was in her element. Her role in mergers and acquisitions was her calling, and she reveled in the leadership position she held and the exceptional team she collaborated with daily. At home, Jennifer was delighted. Her family was her sanctuary, where she refueled, unwound, and found comfort in the chaotic rhythms of their busy life together.

Jennifer was aware that as her children grew older, so did her parents, and the balance Jennifer sought between her professional ambitions and her devotion to family began to weigh heavily on her. She yearned to be an active participant in the lives of those she held dear, to be present in their joys, and to be available to lend support during challenges.

But she couldn't help but wonder—did she need to choose between her flourishing career and her beloved family? Her mother had devoted herself entirely to home life until Jennifer entered high school, after which she engaged in a flurry of volunteer work and part-time jobs. But Jennifer had always envisioned that she'd ascend the corporate ladder. Now she grappled with the ever-increasing demands of her home life, even with a supportive partner.

Balance, once a concept she had assumed she'd master, now seemed like it might be a fantasy. Jennifer questioned if it was possible to maintain equilibrium in the whirlwind of her life. She yearned to know: was there a way to juggle her dreams for her career and the desires of her heart without compromising either?

Is Balance a Myth?

If you're a woman reading this book, there's a good chance you're grappling with your own version of this dilemma. Perhaps you're at the outset of your career, seeking a delicate balance between your professional responsibilities and nurturing a satisfying, healthy lifestyle. Or maybe you find yourself on the brink of a career advancement, weighing the decision's potential unintended costs. And then there are those like Jennifer and me, women whose children are no longer in the crib but who now confront the delicate juggling act of caring for aging parents.

In 2018, LinkedIn conducted a survey involving one thousand working adults to unearth the challenges they faced. The findings were telling—a whopping 38 percent of respondents cited the elusive quest for work-life balance as their most significant challenge.[25] Fast-forward to the postpandemic era, and the struggle to strike that balance has become even more elusive.

With the advent of hybrid work arrangements and the increasing opportunities for remote work, both men and women are yearning for a healthier equilibrium between their work and home life, yet they still grapple to attain it in workplace cultures designed around total commitment. McKinsey & Company's "Women in the Workplace 2023" report found that almost two-thirds of women under the age of thirty say they would be more eager to pursue advancement in their careers if they saw the work-life balance they desire reflected in senior management.[26]

Professional success and a healthy home life are often framed as binary choices. Traditional wisdom has, for the most part, perpetuated the notion that one must choose between a thriving career and a contented family life. This rigid black-and-white perspective places women in particular at the heart of a challenging dilemma, considering the fact that in virtually every culture, women continue to bear the lion's share of family responsibilities.

> *Professional success and a healthy home life are often framed as binary choices.*

No matter which route you opt for, this choice often comes with a lingering internal anxiety that you might have made the wrong decision. If you opt to advance in your career, you fret about how your family might be affected by this choice. On the other hand, if you decide to devote a period to raising your children or pursuing a career without aggressive advancement, you might worry about being disadvantaged when it's time to concentrate more on your professional ambitions.

On top of this inner turmoil are pressures from your family, culture, and even workplace, all with their own preferred course of action. It can feel like a no-win situation. Work or family is an intensely personal choice, and there is no one-size-fits-all solution to the incredibly personal circumstances and needs that each woman must weigh for herself, her family, and the life stage she is in.

Indra Nooyi, the first female CEO of PepsiCo, grappled with these very dilemmas. She grew up in a traditional, conservative Brahmin family in India and went on to serve as the CEO of PepsiCo for twelve of her twenty-four years with the company. In her parting letter to the company employees in 2018, Indra was transparent about the difficulties she felt when choosing between work or family.[27] In an interview with the Aspen Institute, she openly acknowledged that there were many times during her quest for balance when she was painfully unsuccessful. She acknowledged that it is rarely possible for women to have a career and homelife that are balanced.[28]

But that doesn't mean women have to abandon their aspirations. In fact, McKinsey & Company found that women are more ambitious than ever, and it is flexibility that is fueling their drive.[29]

Integration, Not Balance

Growing up in China, both my parents had to work because we needed both their incomes to make ends meet. However, I never felt like I was missing out because my mother worked. Both of my parents' examples shaped my work ethic, resourcefulness, and ingenuity in ways that would not have been the same if we had financial excess or if I had a parent at home with me. It was their love, acceptance, and encouragement that shaped my ambition much more than economics.

Whenever my parents managed to find some time off work, they would come to the village where I lived to be with me. I remember one visit when my mother arrived with a tiny toy oven she had crafted from a piece of metal. She had noticed that I spent my days making pretend pies out of mud with my friends, so she thoughtfully spent her time apart from me crafting a toy that would enhance my playtime, using what she had at hand.

Growing up with financial constraints but abundant love oriented my inner compass and made my priorities clear. My guiding principle was to make choices that would allow me to live a fully integrated life, to be both a professional and a devoted wife and mother.

Notice I said *integrated*, not *balanced*.

The word *balance* implies a state of equilibrium and a trade-off between one thing or another, adhering to the "either-or" notion of conventional wisdom. *Integration* implies coordination and blending. Both of these concepts recognize that a woman's life has seasons and her priorities can shift from day to day, week to week, and year to year.

My guiding principle does not require me to think in terms of "either-or" and make a work-life trade-off. Instead, I make a trade-off between what I can afford to lose and what I cannot.

That's not to say it's easy.

In the early stages of my career, I became a mother to two young daughters. This guided me to channel my energy more toward my family than climbing corporate

> *My guiding principle does not require me to think in terms of "either-or" and make a work-life trade-off. Instead, I make a trade-off between what I can afford to lose and what I cannot.*

ladders, which would come with additional responsibilities and less time with my family. This period wasn't about lack of ambition—quite the opposite.

Even without formal leadership roles, I remained highly engaged at work. I dedicated much of my time to learning every aspect of the FedEx business—from customer experiences to operations, processes, technologies, domestic and international shipping, and more. Like a bamboo, I was growing my career roots without diverting my attention from my daughters and husband.

It wasn't an easy decision or period in my life. I often encountered the prevailing "either-or" thinking, which filled me with doubts. I wondered if I was making a mistake with my career and worried that I might never have the chance to move up the corporate ladder. But at the end of the day, my compass always guided me back to the decision I had made.

I kept telling myself I could always pick up my career later, but I wouldn't be able to reclaim the precious time I'd miss during my children's formative years. Looking back, I can now smile and say that I made the right choice. I was able to have both—a wonderful family and a successful career. But it wasn't that obvious during the process. I had to constantly remind myself of my priorities and principles in life and continue the journey, much like the slogan "Keep calm and carry on."

For me, career success may come and go, but family will always be my number one priority. The choices I made aren't for everyone, and I would never prescribe this path to someone else, as this juggling act is a highly personal decision that you must make based on your unique circumstances.

I want to acknowledge that women in low-income families, single mothers, or those with unsupportive spouses may feel less freedom to make these types of decisions. I want to encourage you that these situations still don't mean you have to settle for a grind that leads to burnout and regret. My parents didn't, and you have more options than they did. Follow the guiding

Follow the guiding principle for your life. It will set your own compass to the north, and you will be on a journey toward living a life you love.

principle for your life. It will set your own compass to the north, and you will be on a journey toward living a life you love.

Prioritize and Grow

Whether you work out of necessity or by choice, a successful career can be a by-product of your fulfilling life. Instead of falling into the "either-or" trap, consider taking a "prioritize-and-grow" approach.

It's a truth we must face: we definitely cannot have it all, but we can make steps toward a more integrated life. Finding your singular orienting principle can help you filter your choices and decisions and line up your commitments and obligations in connection to what matters most to you. Once you have done that, growing both your practical strategies and mindset will get you closer to integration.

Adopt a Seasonal Perspective

Throughout your life and career, priorities shift as you enter different stages. Not everything needs to be a top priority simultaneously. Life is a long journey, and we experience various circumstances and seasons. It's okay to dedicate a significant period to your family, whether it's for pregnancy or taking care of aging parents. During these times, you can continue growing your strengths, finding creative ways to apply your skills, and pushing your limits to become even more valuable than before, even if you step back from or temporarily leave the workforce.

Your path to success might not be a straightforward ascent, but with determination and resilience, and by never giving up on the things that matter most to you, you'll always be one step closer.

Purge Perfection

The pressure to achieve perfection affects women of all ages. Social media encourages us to curate what appears to be a flawless life: perfect bodies, families, homes, diets, and careers all seamlessly in sync. But in reality, no one can excel in every role they play, and that's perfectly fine. Instead of striving for perfection, go with the flow of life and work toward harmony. Give where you can and allow yourself to relax your expectations of yourself in other areas. Life is a journey. What you choose to focus on will be different in different stages. Just be sure to focus on what you can't afford to lose, not what you can!

Cancel Comparison

Comparing yourself to others can lead to internal turmoil and hinder your clarity, direction, and progress toward your goals and dreams. Each woman's situation is

Life is a journey. What you choose to focus on will be different in different stages. Just be sure to focus on what you can't afford to lose, not what you can!

unique, based on her family, relationships, circumstances, skills, ambitions, and desires. There's no one-size-fits-all solution to the challenge of balancing work and personal life. What another woman is doing with her life isn't inherently right or wrong; it's simply her path. Embrace your uniqueness, and chart your own course.

Team Effort

Being a mother is a full-time job. Being an employee is a full-time job. Therefore, pursuing a career and having a fulfilling personal life is a team effort. It certainly was in mine. I could never have done it without the commitment, cooperation, and generosity of my supportive husband. It's crucial to align with your partner on what works best for your goals and objectives during this particular phase of life. Discuss what each family member, including your children, needs to contribute to make this balance possible. Many highly successful individuals attribute their achievements to having support systems.

Ask for Help

Support systems are established when you learn to ask for help. This support can come from a partner who takes on more household responsibilities, assistance from extended family, or even help from a team at work. There's no shame in not being able to be everywhere at once or do everything yourself. You're human. Interestingly, asking for help actually makes you look more competent to those you're asking.[30] Maybe you are on a work trip and your daughter needs a homecoming outfit. Reach out to a friend's mother who loves shopping or fashion, and ask her if she will let your daughter join them on their shopping trip. Asking for help reduces your stress and the chances of regret.[31]

Build Independence

Your value as a mother is not in how much you are able to do for your family. That perspective leads to burnout, resentment, and trouble. Children thrive when given autonomy and responsibility. With training, kids can make meals, do household chores, and run errands for the family. This teaches them cooperation and gives them independence and confidence, skills they will need to navigate the world on their own. Sure, it won't always be seamless, and your urge to take over might be strong, but resist the temptation to become helicopter parents. Let your children learn from their minor mistakes. These experiences are

> *For all of us, integrating our personal and professional dreams requires intentionality and focus.*

what allow them to develop and flourish at their own pace. In this scenario, think of yourself as the farmer tending to the bamboo, nurturing its growth and resilience.

For all of us, integrating our personal and professional dreams requires intentionality and focus. It requires front-end work to equip your team at work and home to support you on your journey. But it's also immensely fulfilling and opens the door to more satisfaction, connection, and fun in the one life you get to live. Rejecting the "either-or" approach to work and life opens the door to creativity, innovation, and flourishing for you, your family, and your team.

In the next chapter, we will dig deeper into the place for fun in your professional life.

CHAPTER TEN

THE HAPPINESS RULE

Alice had it all—a prestigious office on the twentieth floor of a stunning skyscraper with panoramic city views. Her corner office had walls of windows on two sides, offering breathtaking views of the city life and the world, yet Alice seldom looked up from her computer screen. Her work had become an all-consuming presence in her life, dominating five, six, and sometimes seven days a week.

Alice and her husband had started their consulting business together, full of dreams and ambitions. She fondly remembered the days when they'd huddled together in a cramped home office, sketching out ideas and business plans and sharing their hopes. But as the business had grown, it seemed to swallow them whole.

Her husband was perpetually on the road, meeting clients and attending trade shows, while Alice remained anchored in the office, overseeing operations and untangling managerial knots.

As she stared at the financial report on her monitor another late evening, Alice couldn't help but wonder, would they ever get to enjoy their work and its rewards?

On their fifteenth wedding anniversary, they should have been clinking glasses on a Caribbean cruise celebrating all they had achieved, but instead, they'd signed the lease on this modern office space.

With every friendly invitation to coffee or yoga she declined, Alice was increasingly aware that her life had become an endless routine of work, deadlines, and responsibilities. She was good at her work, but she didn't love it. She didn't enjoy being "the boss" as much as she thought she would, and she missed ideating and creating tools and solutions that her customers needed. Even though their business was growing well, she felt like they were always scrambling after different milestones, in pursuit of the next level.

Alice was beginning to feel like she was always chasing a moving target. The constant grind and pressure she felt left no space in her schedule for things like cruises, or even full weekends off.

She closed the financial report and clicked open her personal investment portfolio. She did some quick calculations in her head and assumed, if all things stayed the same, they could sell the company and retire comfortably in about ten years. Then they'd be able to do what she dreamed about.

But to Alice, ten years felt like an eternity. Her mother had died of a heart attack at fifty-five. Her father-in-law had gotten cancer at sixty-three. There had to be a better way to live life than chasing one goal after the next.

She turned off her computer and noticed the bright-orange sunset painting the sky outside her window and casting

> *She realized joy, beauty, and fulfillment didn't have to wait for some distant day in the future. She could find happiness in each moment along the way.*

a golden glow on the buildings around her. She wondered if they always looked this beautiful out her window. As she paused to take in the scene, a question crept into her mind:

How many of these sunsets have I missed as I've been sitting at my desk trying to hit the next goal?

She knew the honest answer was probably, *Quite a few.*

In that moment, something profoundly shifted inside Alice. She realized she had to think differently about her professional journey. She realized joy, beauty, and fulfillment didn't have to wait for some distant day in the future. She could find happiness in each moment along the way. As she took her coat off the coat rack and put it on, picked up her purse, and purposefully left her briefcase behind, she felt hopeful and encouraged by the possibility but wondered how she would do it.

Life Is Short

In our professional culture, there's a prevailing philosophy often touted as the key to success: "Grind now, play later." This is the notion that says you should devote your working years to tirelessly focusing on accumulating external accomplishments and milestones. The implied result is that if you work hard enough and long enough, you'll eventually reach a point where you don't have to work anymore, and then you can savor the rewards of your labor.

This "grind now, play later" mentality defers gratification to some distant point in the future. It also assumes a linear nature to your career trajectory, steadily climbing up one single ladder and consistently reaching smaller milestones on your way to the top.

It leaves most professionals with a pervasive mindset of needing to perform, prove oneself, and position oneself for earning more money, promotions, and more significant next-level accomplishments. It also implies that ending your career somewhere other than the top is a failure, and since every company only has a few people at the top, that is a limiting way to view success for the vast majority of workers.

Society pressures us to measure our success through external metrics like money, status, and possessions. When we do, it creates downward pressure on our day-to-day performance and puts us on the hamster wheel of constant striving for transactional rewards. This constant state of striving creates discontent, dissatisfaction, disconnection, and

> *It is hard to feel happy and fulfilled when you're constantly chasing the next external goal you've set (or has been set for you).*

at times, despair. You spend your days busily working, hoping that one day you might reach the point where you can finally relax, find happiness, and have "fun."

It is hard to feel happy and fulfilled when you're constantly chasing the next external goal you've set (or has been set for you). Doing that will only bring you stress and anxiety. Whatever your position, salary, or status, there is always someone who has risen just a little higher or earned a little more. External validation of income, status, and other people's positive opinion of you is not the goal to orient yourself by.

Don't Wait

What are the perils of endlessly grinding now and hoping for future happiness? Regret, frustration, and dreams deferred. I asked a retired CEO what he regretted in his hugely successful and lucrative career. He told me he regretted not slowing down to smell the roses along the way. He worked nonstop for forty years and never took the time to enjoy the places he traveled or the people he met. He was only focused on the deals he was there to make, not enjoyment, happiness, or celebrating his achievements.

Similarly, my father's retirement at age seventy-five brought its own set of struggles. Having been engrossed in his profession for so long, he grappled with disconnecting from it mentally. Although he ceased office visits, his mind remained firmly embedded in work. This transition made it challenging to rekindle interests and joys.

Another poignant warning comes from a story my friend told me about a couple whose careers had consumed their lives. They wanted to travel, but they had no time. Upon retirement, they booked a trip to South America and were off to climb some ancient Mayan ruins. But as they arrived at their dream destination and eyed the steep stairs to the top of the temple ruins, they realized they physically couldn't make the climb. Instead, they handed their camera to a younger traveler and asked him to take a picture from the top for them.

Grinding now and playing later comes with serious risks. Why gamble on something as important as your happiness?

The truth is, money and status are simply not enough to paint your life with vibrant colors of happiness.

How to Have Fun

The truth is, money and status are simply not enough to paint your life with vibrant colors of happiness. They may buy you pleasurable experiences and afford you financial flexibility, but it is insufficient to support a life of happiness and fulfillment. This realization is pivotal because it underscores that the hope and potential of financial freedom or fun experiences in retirement are not enough to fuel you for all the work that awaits you in the days and years preceding that.

Instead of external measures that may or may not lead to a point where you're financially comfortable, what if you asked this question along the way: *Am I happy?*

You will spend one-third of your life at work.[32] Consider some more perspective on that. The average life expectancy for a woman in the United States has decreased to only seventy-six years.[33] Life is, quite simply, short.

I'm not advocating you quit your job and solely pursue things that bring you pleasure. I'm suggesting that you think differently. What if your pursuit of success doesn't need to be a relentless grind toward happiness? What if your pursuit was toward happiness, including in your professional life?

The rule says, "Grind now, be happy later." I say, "Be as happy as you possibly can along the way!"

Richard Branson built his empire on this very idea. "The best advice I could possibly give you is that you've got to have fun. You've got to be happy. You never want to have a billion-dollar business to have a trillion-dollar headache. If there's any one person out there I know that is miserable, most of them are billionaires. They forgot how to have fun!"[34]

Last year I had the opportunity to tour the Getty Center in Brentwood, California. The beautiful art museum is part of the legacy that John Paul Getty Sr. left. Getty was a petroleum industrialist, and in 1966, *The Guinness Book of World Records* named him the world's wealthiest private citizen.

At the time of his death in 1976, he was worth an estimated $23 billion in today's dollars. Amidst the grandeur, there was a striking picture on the wall depicting Mr. Getty and his wife (one of the five he had). They wore expressions of profoundly unhappy individuals. Intrigued, I delved deeper after the tour and discovered the truth: Mr. Getty was one of those immensely wealthy but deeply unhappy souls. I also learned that the Getty family's "curse" of misery, relationship struggles, and hardships has continued in his family line through the years.[35]

Life is too short to be miserable for a paycheck or prestige. More money and status alone won't weave the fabric of a fulfilling, happy life.

As I started my career, my aspirations were initially only set on becoming a managing director. However, my growth has far exceeded that desire. I am a senior officer of a Fortune 50 global company and sit on two public boards. My achievements have surpassed my expectations because success for success's sake was never my aim.

As the Gettys can tell you, status and money aren't enough to be happy.

Today I don't feel the need to prove myself to others, and I don't feel stress and anxiety to accomplish even more. Instead, my focus is on enjoying what I've accomplished, focusing on paying it forward and helping others be successful, which only compounds the joy and fulfillment I've already experienced in my life.

Maya Angelou said, "You can only become truly accomplished at something you love. Don't make money your goal. Instead, pursue the things you love doing, and then do them so well that people can't take their eyes off you."

In my life, one of the keys to having fun and finding happiness has been finding alignment between my passions and strengths and my role in the company. My job in technology and innovation is something I am passionate about because it's creating change, not just function execution.

In this position, I get to use my strengths to help shape the future of FedEx operations through the use of fascinating emerging technologies like robotics and autonomous vehicles. When passion and strengths align with the job, work becomes fun, interesting, and engaging. For me, going to the office doesn't even feel like work. It's like being paid to do the things I like.

> *When passion and strengths align with the job, work becomes fun, interesting, and engaging.*

Here are five key things to do to find the most happiness, joy, and fulfillment in your career:

Clarify Your Passions

The best feeling in the world is getting paid to do what you love. When you pursue your passion, you will likely enjoy what you do. Enjoyment and happiness allow you to be both the most creative and most productive, and because of that, you will also likely find a high degree of success in your career.

External success is the result of the internal objective of pursuing your passion. When you genuinely enjoy your work, it fuels your happiness and fulfillment, and though it's still work, you have fun while you do it.

You must uncover the type of work that resonates with your true self the most. A master chef will tirelessly perfect their dishes, a designer will invest in crafting fresh designs, and an artist will dedicate months to completing one masterpiece. Their passion fuels their work, and yours should too. Not only will you be happier, but those around you will be as well.

Set Intangible Goals

In *The Infinite Game* by Simon Sinek, the author identifies the only true competitor we have is ourselves, not the Joneses. We don't need to try and outdo others in what we achieve or earn to find happiness. We need to adopt a continuous improvement mindset so that we are always getting better.

This thinking contributes to satisfaction, fulfillment, and direction. If you make your goals about money, you will never have enough. But if you view life as an infinite game to get better, be happier, and be more fulfilled, it's about constant growth, just like the bamboo.

Everyone makes different decisions about work and life, and the key question to ask is, "Are you enjoying it?" When a person is doing the things they love, it often leads to a sense of satisfaction and less of a burden or burnout. Conversely, the opposite is true. Material things or transactional goals will likely never end, so instead, chase something meaningful out of passion or purpose.

Define *Enough*

One of my favorite books is *The Psychology of Money* by Morgan Housel. In this book, Housel tells the story of an opulent yacht party where the guests were billionaires, celebrities, and wildly successful individuals. Among them, there was a writer. People asked the writer how he felt to be in such a group as this, with staggering wealth and power.

His response was striking. He said, "I feel perfectly content because I have something they don't. I have *enough*." Having enough gave him contentment, confidence, and peace to live the life he had and not desire the things that other people had or were chasing. Think about your life, and define what having *enough* might look like to you. When you can hone in on that, you can stop chasing success and money just for the sake of more because you already have enough.

Celebrate Your Wins

Along your journey, celebrate your large and small accomplishments. Recently, I attended an exclusive mobility summit hosted by an elite consulting firm. Everyone there was considered to be very successful. In a warm-up exercise, the facilitator laid out glossy postcards with various images on them. We were asked to pick two cards, one to depict our current state of mind and the other to show our future desired state.

Inevitably, most people picked images that illustrate frustra-

> *Taking time to celebrate wins gives you proper perspective and gratitude, and it allows you time to prepare for the growth still to come.*

tions and challenges as the first postcard and images that depict happiness, relaxation, and success as the second postcard. The card I chose with my current state had a lovely picture of a white sand beach and hammock; the second one was a picture of a hot-air balloon.

This high-performing group was astonished that my current state could be represented by the image of the beach and hammock. But I explained that in the past eighteen months, I'd earned a promotion and two board of directors seats. I wanted to take time to celebrate this first before moving on to my next goal. If I didn't, I would be like a hamster on the wheel, just chasing the next goal and never taking time to see just how far I'd run. Taking time to celebrate wins gives you proper perspective and gratitude, and it allows you time to prepare for the growth still to come.

Whether you find yourself at the dawn of your career or in the midst of it, the pursuit of professional happiness remains an open avenue. If you're just embarking on your professional journey, you have the golden opportunity to liberate yourself from the "grind now" mindset and explore various jobs, functions, and even entire industries that bring harmony to both your occupation and your strengths and passions.

For those in the midst of their careers, there are indeed unique considerations to be weighed, extenuating circumstances you will need to consider—such as financial flexibility, time, and skills needed. However, these circumstances shouldn't thwart your quest for joy and fulfillment. Pivoting to a life of happiness, even in midcareer, is possible for you. It might necessitate more meticulous planning and preparation, but it's no less feasible. Your pursuit of happiness doesn't have an expiration date.

Stop Competing against Others

I never compete with my professional peers. The only person I compete with is myself. When you compare and compete, you create anxiety and scarcity. Success becomes a win-or-lose proposition. But with the mindset that there is enough space for everyone to win, your professional endeavors can become a win-win for you and others and a fulfilling, happy, expansive professional experience for everyone.

Don't Go at It Alone

In the landscape of corporate America, there's an independent self-sufficient ethos to the culture. Yet my conviction stands firm: "A rising tide lifts all boats." As we genuinely engage with, connect to, and uplift those in our professional sphere, the joy multiplies, and success becomes a shared venture.

My personal achievements are the outcome of my dedication, creativity, and willingness to think differently. However, the happiness derived from these accomplishments is not solitary; it's amplified by the people I'm fortunate to share it with.

My corporate journey was supported by my mentors and sponsors who played pivotal roles. These connections weren't transactional or borne out of a desire for personal gain. Instead, they were rooted in mutual respect, appreciation, and genuine human connection. These mentors generously shared their time and wisdom, unthreatened by the ascent of a younger female colleague.

This idea of mutual growth should permeate every rung of the corporate ladder. Each level is teeming with individuals who can inspire and enrich your journey, just as they can benefit from your wisdom, strengths, and experiences.

In my days as a manager, casual lunches with a senior vice president were a source of genuine connection rather than a calculated career move for me. Our exchanges over sandwiches in the company cafeteria became a symbiotic relationship, where I became his sounding board and he, in turn, fostered my executive acumen.

This principle doesn't only apply when looking up the corporate ladder. Treating everyone with kindness, curiosity, and interest, regardless of title, is paramount. Every colleague is a human being deserving of respect; we simply do different jobs within the same company. Those differences don't assign more or less value to a person based on the potential future advantages they may offer you.

Take Lesa Wood for instance. Lesa has been an executive assistant in my current department since 2007. In our time together, we gradually became friends, and for seventeen years, she's had a front-row seat to witnessing my career. She's been a source of encouragement and celebration, and when I became corporate vice president, she stepped into the role of my personal executive assistant. Our working relationship has a foundation of personal interest and friendship. I can't overstate what a blessing it is to be supported by someone I can trust completely and who always has my best interests in mind.

A wise friend recently remarked, "You need people in your life who think you're a big deal." To achieve that, you must be present, be seen, and invest in those around you while allowing them to invest in you. In doing so, you'll find support, connection, and much more happiness than if you had to go at it alone.

Both Yin and Yang

The yin and yang symbol represents the Chinese philosophy of interconnected and balanced forces. The yin and yang are complementary forces that mutually perpetuate a dynamic system where the sum is greater than either part; both are needed.

This idea is helpful to think about. We've discussed both setting goals and pushing limits and having fun, celebrating wins, and finding happiness in your journey. You can't *only* pursue fun because doing so is unrealistic among the physical and relational realities of life. You also can't *only* pursue goals and success either though. You will never find true satisfaction or enjoyment because chasing goals means the finish line is constantly moving further down the field. You must have balance. You must do both.

Goals are important to have, but don't chase endless ones. Define what *enough* is, get clarity on your passions, and celebrate what you've already achieved with the people you enjoy.

Work does not have to be a grind. It really can feel like fun each day. When you align your vocation with your strengths, opportunities, and goals, you will feel connected, authentic, engaged, and inspired.

To get there, you must answer the most important question: "What does success look like to me?" This is the question we will explore in the next chapter.

CHAPTER ELEVEN

TOUCHSTONE

G iven the challenges of my childhood, my parents' sole aspiration for me was that I grow up and be happy in whatever I found to do. For them, my happiness equated success. This perspective profoundly shaped my mindset about my life and freed me from the conventional pressures and expectations of a traditional path to success. It empowered me to explore the opportunities that truly resonated with my desires.

As an adult, the pursuit of happiness remains a central pillar in my personal definition of success. This is not a self-indulgent or self-centered pursuit but a guiding principle for my journey. That doesn't mean every day has been easy; there have been times of deep distress and frustration. However, during challenging times, I've been able to innovate and persevere because my life is anchored to my own values and goals, not someone else's.

With happiness as my compass to guide me, I've taken risks and had adventures. I haven't been forced to make a binary choice between my career or my family, and I've been able to choose pleasure over profit.

Unfortunately, not many people have experienced this same freedom. Because it brings me great happiness to help others find this freedom and unlock unanticipated success, the remaining pages of this book are designed to help you do just that.

REDEFINING SUCCESS

In the professional realm, many people—intentionally or unintentionally guided by the implicit rules—focus their careers and lives toward amassing wealth and status. They chase after the unspoken promises that this pursuit eventually will lead to a life of ease, comfort, and security. However, true happiness is never found when you're living your life by someone else's rules or working toward their definition of success.

Happiness is a deeply personal journey arising from self-awareness, intentional choices, decisions, priorities, and circumstances. It's not found on the other side of a lifetime of accomplished transactional goals. It's not tied to family or children or bank account balances. It cannot be measured by external benchmarks at all. Happiness, fundamentally, begins with you. The pivotal starting point on this journey is to unravel the rules that have shaped your choices. Peel back the layers of external and internal expectations, and begin to create a path toward your own definition of what success means to you.

WHAT SUCCESS MEANS TO *YOU*

When you define what success means to you, you are freed from the implicit forces guiding you toward an unfulfilling destination. You take control of your own future and your own happiness. But perhaps you're in a stage of your career where you feel like you're just surviving. Perhaps you're still learning the ropes of your job or trying to get a better sense of your interests and strengths. Defining success, even as you're just beginning your journey, will help you chart a course that you can be proud of and happy with. It will offer you a touchstone to orient your choices along the way.

Perhaps you know you have been working hard toward a goal that no longer fits you. You're aware that implicit expectations have, up to this point, guided your choices. You may feel stuck and unsure of how (and when) to make a change. When you get clarity on your own definition of success, you gain authenticity, empowerment, and joy in the journey.

Maybe circumstances in your life are causing you to make a pivot you didn't anticipate, and the idea of success feels even farther from your reach. Remember the bamboo: you are always growing, even if the growth is imperceptible. Defining what success means to you signifies that your growth will be in the right direction when it does finally come.

Stalls and setbacks are similar to what happens to the bamboo when a stalk gets cut. Instead of spending energy trying to grow more roots to regain the lost height, the bamboo simply unfurls new leaves. Those new leaves send energy down to the existing roots so the plant can grow new shoots. In fact, cutting the bamboo stimulates its growth. Setbacks, mistakes, delays, and detours can do the same for you!

Growth and resilience are within you. Making the commitment of bringing clarity to your definition of success is the first step to new growth.

CULTIVATING CLARITY

China is famous for its elaborate gardens. These gardens are living artworks, masterpieces of design and symbolism. Rooted in principles of yin and yang, balance, order, beauty, and exploration, these spaces host symbolic plantings of bamboo, plum blossoms, and pine trees that represent resilience, endurance, and longevity. Architectural elements like pavilions, teahouses, and bridges make inviting spaces for people to rest and reflect in the beauty. Yet the true essence lies in the paths that meander through the scenery, beckoning visitors to not only observe but to experience the garden.

Like these Chinese gardens, the lessons of this book are to be experienced, not simply observed. What follows is an invitation to embark on your own journey to find clarity, direction, and success for yourself. It is a pathway of contemplation and self-discovery to identify more of who you are and uncover the meaning of success for you.

As you proceed through the rest of this chapter, you will encounter a series of questions designed to unveil the implicit rules shaping your life and bring you to a new sense of clarity and direction. Through these exercises, you'll pinpoint your goals, recognize your strengths, spot opportunities, and identify the limitations that either guide you or obstruct your progress.

This isn't simple work. It requires introspection and time, a commitment I encourage you to make. Like strolling through a Chinese garden, there will be moments that cause you to pause and reflect. There is no need to rush. There is no looming deadline. There's no assignment due at 8:00 a.m. tomorrow.

Take all the time you need. Let this experience unfold on its own time—over days, weeks, or even months—so you can emerge with a comprehensive understanding of your aspirations and strengths, and be prepared and oriented for the growth that awaits.

The following section is intended for you to spend time in reflection and record your thoughts in a journal or notebook. Then, when it's time to create your Touchstone, you can use the designed spaces in the book to fill in your thoughts.

Creating Your Garden

The rest of this chapter will guide you on your own journey to create your own beautiful garden: a visual, personal representation of what a successful life means for you.

Just as every life is distinct, so too will be the garden you cultivate. Engage with the prompts, questions, and reflection exercises that follow thoughtfully, and you will begin to clarify what success—and, ultimately, happiness—looks like for you.

At the center of the garden will be a Touchstone. This will serve as your grounding point, a place to come back to in moments of challenge and opportunity, to gain clarity, reorientation, and confirmation. Let the garden and your Touchstone guide you to tranquility amid life's storms. Let it be a compass, leading you forward as you pursue your vision and your version of a fulfilling and successful life.

The illustrations that follow offer a visual recap of the rules we explored in this book. They will move you toward transforming the seeds of your greatness into a flourishing garden—rooted, authentic, and irresistibly satisfying.

THE GOAL RULE

Start with you.

You can't build a successful life until you invest in yourself. The Goal Rule says to plant the seeds that will bear fruit in your life and nurture them so they start to grow.

THE STRENGTH RULE

Lean into your strengths.

You have strengths, and you have struggles. This is normal. The Strength Rule says to lean into your strengths and help them grow. Some of the seeds you plant will begin to take root; others won't. Nurture those that do.

THE OPPORTUNITY RULE

Focus on possibilities.

It's human nature to look for threats and obstacles. You must train yourself to look for opportunities. The Opportunity Rule says to focus on possibilities. This doesn't mean you ignore the obstacles; it simply means you push forward where it makes sense. It's here that your seeds break through the soil and push toward the light.

THE LIMITS RULE

Thrive in challenges.

Anything worth doing requires hard work, grit, and determination. The Limits Rule says that challenges make you stronger. Learn to lean into the wind, embrace the criticism, and thrive in challenging times. This is how the smallest plants begin to grow into resilient stalks.

THE EITHER-OR RULE

Integrate the essentials.

Life is more than just you, your work, or your family. It's a blend of all that makes you happy. The Either-Or Rule says to integrate the essentials. You must stop worrying about everyone else and focus on your essentials. Invest in those things, and they'll begin to thrive.

THE HAPPINESS RULE

Enjoy the journey.

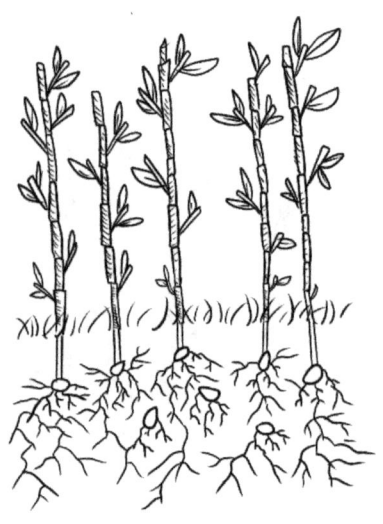

You don't enter a garden to quickly get to the exit. You meander, stroll, and linger at the places that make you happy. The Happiness Rule says to enjoy the journey. Life isn't a race. It isn't a destination. Put down deep roots into the things that matter. Surround yourself with the essentials. Enjoy the journey.

HOW TO BUILD YOUR GARDEN

A garden is a peaceful place, but when you look closely, it's fully alive. There is a time for movement, a time to be still, and a time to reflect. That blend of movement and stillness will guide your journey.

OBSERVE

When you encounter the word *observe* and this icon, it signals a moment to step back in time. Reflect on the paths you've taken, the lessons you've learned, and the growth you've gained. This isn't meant to be a linear process; you have liberty to choose the prompts that resonate with you most at this moment. Let the ebb and flow of observation guide you along this reflective journey.

EXPLORE

When you encounter the term *explore* and this icon, engage with the focused and purposeful prompts tailored to guide you in unraveling the layers of self-discovery and onward toward true happiness.

☀ ANTICIPATE

Whenever you see the word *anticipate* and this icon appear, begin crafting the statements that form the shape of your garden. These statements will compose the Touchstone you create at the end of this chapter.

I will be your guide as you navigate the intricacies of each rule for yourself, and based on people I've spoken with, I've written a variety of different examples to show you how your responses might look. Let's begin the journey. So grab your journal or notebook, and let's begin the journey.

THE GOAL RULE

Start with you.

To begin to grow, you must go back to the beginning. Just as a bamboo springs from a seed to a sprout, your journey begins with you. Growing your self-awareness through self-discovery is essential. It is only when you know who you are that you can set goals for yourself that align with your values, not external standards.

👀 OBSERVE

- ► What gifts and talents did you have as a child that you have left unexplored?

- ► What activities, hobbies, or projects absorbed your time, attention, and creativity? How did those activities make you feel? Why do you think they brought you such joy?

- ► What activities or hobbies do you engage in today that bring you to that same state of absorbed joy?

- ► Revisit the role models or heroes of your youth. What qualities did they possess that you admired?

► Recall a challenge or fear you overcame as a child. What did that experience teach you about yourself? How has it empowered you today?

► What principles, philosophies, religions, or ideologies are most important to you? How do these shape your perspective on life, success, and happiness today?

 EXPLORE

► **Discover your joy.** Write as many statements or short paragraphs as you'd like about the kinds of things that fill you with joy. Make these present tense.

Some prompts to guide you:

» *I am filled with joy when I cook a good meal for my family and we sit around the table talking and laughing together.*

» *I am filled with joy when I help a client achieve their objectives and they let me know how much my expertise means to them.*

» *I am filled with joy when I sit in my comfortable chair, with a cup of steaming green tea in hand, and read a good book that takes me to another world.*

► **Write a description of your *true* self.** Picture yourself at your absolute best without the constraints of who you think you *should* be or what other people think. Lean into your innate understanding of yourself.

Example:

» *The true me loves the outdoors. I find strength and peace when I am with nature. Hiking by a stream in the mountains lets me clear my head and get in touch with my thoughts. Standing with my feet in the ocean reminds me of how small I am and how big the world is. The true me is highly independent and values autonomy. I love working with people, but I also like to chart my own course and pursue things that interest me. At my best, I have plenty of time for input in the form of reading, podcasts, and captivating conversations. I also have flexibility to work on things that matter to me and tie back to the things I loved to do as a child.*

► **Jettison others' goals.** Reflect on goals others set for you, whether implicitly or explicitly. What were they? How did you receive those messages? What would happen if you were liberated from those messages, reclaimed your autonomy, and defined your own aspirations?

☀ ANTICIPATE

Review your responses and distill the top three "seeds" you wish to nurture. Turn the most important ones into "I will" statements.

Example:

» *I will invest in my gift of warmth and sense of humor to encourage others. Every time they engage with me, I will have made their lives better.*

» *I will use my ability to connect unconnected things and bring unique and innovative solutions to life for the people I serve.*

» *I will continue to be a learner, surrounding myself with positive voices and great books, so I can feed my sense of wonder and ideation.*

▶ Your Seeds:

THE STRENGTH RULE

Lean into your strengths.

Directing your energy toward your strengths will amplify your capabilities and unique assets, setting you apart and adding value to others while enhancing your enjoyment of your life. While acknowledging your weaknesses is essential, dwelling on them is counterproductive. Instead, focus on recognizing, understanding, and leveraging your strengths to cultivate a more joyful and fulfilling life.

👀 OBSERVE

► Are you prone to dwelling on your weaknesses or focusing on your strengths? What factors contribute to this tendency? Has this tendency served you well in your life?

► How comfortable are you discussing your strengths and sharing them openly?

- ► Identify activities (personal and professional) that come naturally to you but others often struggle with. Delve into the answer thoroughly as most people overlook these things about themselves and assume everyone can do them.

- ► Analyze a recent success and pinpoint what abilities, gifts, or advantages helped you achieve it.

- ► Reflect on what activities make you feel most energized or fulfilled? How do those align with your strengths?

- ► Recall instances when you felt most proud of your work or efforts. Describe these times in detail. Detail the skills these instances required and why you think using them brings you joy.

- ► Consider one area of struggle in which you've spent significant time trying to correct. What would it do to your focus, time, and energy if you no longer focused on that area and worked on developing a strength instead?

EXPLORE

- ► **Brag on yourself.** Write a paragraph celebrating all the ways you are amazing. This is a personal reflection to be honest about you being exceptional.

- ▶ **Get an outside opinion.** Seek feedback from trusted colleagues, friends, or family about what they perceive as your exceptional strengths. Let these people know why you are looking for this feedback: you want to use it to get even better in those areas.

- ▶ **Develop a particular strength.** Select a particular strength that makes you exceptional, and outline ways you can enhance and develop it further. Consider seeking a coach or mentor, invest in training, read books, or listen to podcasts. Push yourself to grow even more in this area.

 ## ANTICIPATE

Use one of these templates to write three declarative statements about your strengths.

- ▶ [Name of a strength] is an area of strength for me. I commit to developing it by _____, _____, and _____.

- ▶ My top strength is _____. I grow that strength by [adding a specific action].

- ▶ I commit to _____ so that I can enhance that strength and leverage it to [add a specific action.]

Example:

» *Wonder and imagination are areas of strength for me. I feed my mind with good inputs, scheduling regular time for thinking and imagination, and look for ways to solve high-level problems.*

» *I look for ways to teach this to others so I can better understand my strength.*

» *I commit to reading three books per month so my mind is full of good thoughts and helpful information.*

► Your Strengths:

THE OPPORTUNITY RULE

Focus on possibilities.

Opportunities are more than a matter of luck or "right place, right time" circumstances. They are about being able to identify the right opportunities, actively shaping and influencing the conditions you find yourself in to create the right opportunities, and taking action when action is warranted. The wrong opportunities have a real opportunity cost to them, so getting clarity on the right opportunities is what this section is for. The right opportunities for you will align with your interests and strengths.

👀 OBSERVE

....

► Recall a moment when a door opened or the perfect opportunity seemed to present itself. Reflect on that time, and identify the work you did that preceded it. How might you duplicate these things to create more opportunities in the future?

► Consider what opportunities you *hope* would come your way. Spend some time thinking about what you *want* to come into your life, and write them here. Naming these things makes them easier to spot when they show up in your life.

► When an opportunity presents itself, how easy or difficult is it for you to embrace it and take action to capitalize on that opportunity? Commit to acting as quickly as possible when an opportunity arises that fits your goals.

► Explore the intersections of your passions, strengths, and goals. What unique opportunities might be found there? Brainstorm various ideas without worrying about how realistic they are. The point of this exercise is to get your "possibility muscle" working.

► Think about the possibilities you have dismissed because they felt too overwhelming. Who could assist you in overcoming these mental barriers and limiting beliefs?

► Review the "opportunities" you have been pursuing. Are there any that, upon reflection, should really be ignored?

◉ EXPLORE

- ▶ **Pay attention to synchronicities.** Synchronicities are things that seem to magically align with your desired path. What surprising occurrences have you noticed happening in your life lately? How might they be linked to your goals? What might happen if you followed these serendipitous signs?

- ▶ **Influence your opportunities.** Think about where you want to go and what you want to do. What are the places, activities, and people you should be surrounding yourself with? Position yourself properly, and more opportunities will unfold.

- ▶ **Conduct an opportunity audit.** Dedicate a week to record every small opportunity you encounter, no matter how insignificant it seems. This includes new connections, invitations, or any novel ideas that cross your mind. In doing so, you will likely change your thinking about the amount of opportunities that truly exist.

☀ ANTICIPATE

When it comes to opportunities, you have the power to make your own luck. Use the Opportunity Rule to unleash the mindset of limitless possibilities. Complete the examples below, and use them to set the right limits that expand what's possible and protect you from chasing opportunities that don't contribute to your happiness.

► I actively pursue opportunities that [insert your specific goals related to your purpose].

► I can create opportunities to help me [insert the way an opportunity might help you reach your goal or develop a strength].

Example:

» *I pursue opportunities that help fulfill my purpose of helping people bring their ideas to life.*

» *I look for ways to listen to others closely and apply my strength of strategy and clarity to their problems.*

» *I create opportunities to help me develop my strength of leadership by sending out a weekly text or email to people I want to mentor.*

THE LIMITS RULE

Thrive in challenges.

In the playbook of conventional wisdom, there's a chapter that says you must know your limits so you can stay within them. While it is valuable to understand your limits, don't allow them to confine or define you. Be aware of your *current* limits, and look for ways to surpass them. There is no assurance of success in staying safely within your limits. In fact, it might be the very thing that leads you to fail.

👀 OBSERVE

....

► How do you personally define limits? Do you see them as restrictive forces or constraints that might actually offer guidance?

► Jot down a list of what you consider to be limits in your life today. What causes you to view these things as limits? Are they actually limits, or do you need to change your thinking?

► Remember a time when you pushed past your limits and achieved something you didn't think was possible. How did that make you feel? How did it alter your perception of those limits from the vantage point of success?

► Identify someone in your circle who seems to live life without much regard for its limits. In what ways do they challenge you or make you uncomfortable? What aspects of their approach would you like to incorporate to your own life?

► Seek out individuals you know (or can learn about) who faced seemingly insurmountable limits and yet thrived and accomplished something worthwhile. If possible, set up a conversation with them, and see what you can learn from their experience.

► What is one goal or hobby you have always wanted to pursue (art, musical instrument, sport) but have listened to the lie that you wouldn't succeed? What if you made a commitment to give it a try anyway?

⊘ EXPLORE

▶ **Push past one limit.** Consider the list above and the limits that feel like constraints upon your life. Identify one, and commit to pushing past that limit. Embrace the inevitable discomfort this commitment brings. Act before you are ready. Do something that scares you. Then reflect on what you learned and how it made you stronger.

▶ **Create the right kind of limits.** Understand that not every limit is a roadblock. Some can be stepping stones for your advancement. Align these constraints with your purpose and objectives. Set limits for your-self—a deadline, a routine, a target, a reward—creat-ing a framework that propels you forward and main-tains your focus.

▶ **Reflect on your growth.** Every difficult thing you have accomplished happened on the other side of your limits. Compile a list of ten significant achieve-ments you have accomplished in your life. For each one, identify the limits you pushed past to reach that accomplishment and where and how you grew as a result.

☀ ANTICIPATE

Write a declaration of limits that you've overcome and how they have made you a stronger person.

> » *I am stronger because I've faced my limits and surpassed them. Growing up as the child of a single mom, we didn't have a lot of opportunities. However, this made everything I worked to accomplish that much sweeter. When I was the first person from my family to walk across the stage and receive my college diploma, I thought of all the times my mom encouraged me to keep going when I wanted to quit, and I realized I will never give up on any of my dreams. My limits won't define me.*

THE EITHER-OR RULE

Integrate the essentials.

You don't need to make a tough choice between a happy personal life or a successful professional life; integration is possible. By deliberately assessing and prioritizing what is essential in this particular phase of your life, purging perfectionism, canceling comparisons, and seeking support, you can make space for a well-rounded life.

👀 OBSERVE

► What would you call "essential" in your life? Why?

► Was keeping "first things first" modeled for you as a young person? What unintentional lessons (both good and bad) did you learn about how to prioritize your life?

- Scrutinize the way you spend your time, your money, and your energy. How closely do these things align with what you have identified as essential?

- Have you made a compromise and made something essential that really shouldn't be? Why?

- Identify one area of your life in which you'd like to be more intentional with your attention or energy. How might you begin to take steps in this direction?

- Think of someone in your life who has done an exceptional job at building a life around their essentials. What can you learn from their example?

EXPLORE

- **Identify your nonnegotiables.** Despite the widespread belief that you can, and should, juggle everything, the truth is, you can't do it all simultaneously. There will always be seasons of life where certain things must take precedence. Identify your nonnegotiables—family, career, hobbies, faith, ambition—and use them to guide the type of garden you are cultivating.

- **Establish the right boundaries.** Just as a garden has clear demarcations, so should your life. Boundaries may feel like constraints, but they are often the keys to staying on course. When contemplating what's essential in your life, boundaries safeguard the things that are important to you. Keeping them safe will allow them to thrive.

► **Consider the opportunity cost.** Every yes you commit to means a multitude of nos. Before committing to something, take a moment to reflect on the opportunity cost. If it's worth the cost and aligns with your priorities, move ahead. However, if it jeopardizes something essential to you, develop the courage to say no.

☀ ANTICIPATE

To find true happiness, identify the essentials that shape your life. Write them as declarations here.

For me to be happy, these are my essentials:

» *Family. My family is the most important thing in my life. I will always prioritize my family and make sure to build strong relationships with my spouse and my children. I want them to know they can always count on me.*

» *Health. I will always make room for exercise so I live a long and full life. For me, that means spending time jogging three to four times per week. I love to start my day with a brisk jog. It helps me clear my head and bring my best to the day ahead.*

» *Travel. I love to see new places. To do that, I will work hard so I can take one big trip each year and several smaller trips to new places. When I'm there, I will take lots of pictures, try new restaurants, and experience new cultures.*

» *Learning. It is essential for me to learn new things, so I will always look for new hobbies, skills, and challenges to keep me sharp and growing.*

THE HAPPINESS RULE

Enjoy the journey.

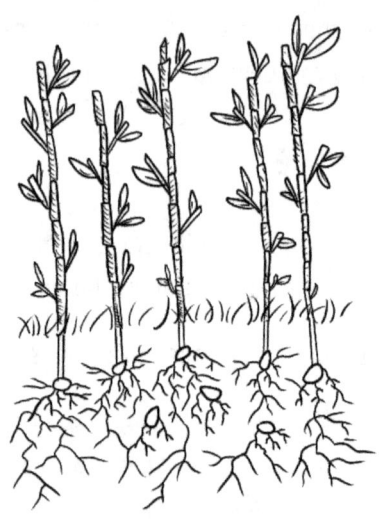

Conventional wisdom says, "Grind now, be happy later." But why not infuse happiness into every step of the journey? That's what the Happiness Rule is all about. It's about building your whole life for your enjoyment, every step of the way. Adopting this mindset guides you to work that resonates with your passion and strengths and brings you deep fulfillment. It disregards others' implicit or explicit expectations of you. It transforms your life into a delightful, courageous adventure, and your work will evolve into captivating and enriching experiences to celebrate.

👀 OBSERVE

► What is your personal definition of happiness? Take your time to delve into this, as many overlook its significance. Linger on this question for a while, and really articulate your personal definition.

► Reflect on the success of your journey so far. Think back over the diverse phases of your life, and consider which parts made you the happiest. What made these instances particularly joyful for you?

► Consider the type of work that brings you intense joy and personal satisfaction. This may be unpaid, volunteer work you do in addition to your occupation. What is it about this work that you love?

► What hobbies, activities, and experiences do you wish to incorporate more into your life? What about these things that make you happy?

► Identify which parts of your life are making you *un*happy. Where do you have the agency to make a change? What might that change be? What might it cost you to make it? What might it cost you not to make it?

► Imagine designing a life around your happiness. What parts of your life would you keep (your essentials), and what parts of your life would you leave behind? What's stopping you from taking action?

◈ EXPLORE

- ► **Search the seasons of your life.** Amid the hustle of daily life, we often forget the many things and people we have to be grateful for. Search the seasons of your life, and reflect on the times when you were the happiest. Seek out subtle hints within those memories for clues about what made you happy, and use those clues to create more seasons like that in the future.

- ► **Perform an honest assessment of your current position.** Examine your work role and your responsibilities now. Assess them to determine whether they contribute to your happiness or possibly detract from it. No situation is perfect every day, but if there are more things that drain you in your work than energize you, it might be a sign that you need a change. Reflect on your definition of happiness, and make sure your work and career are in alignment.

- ► **Write your obit (a memorial statement).** This exercise holds profound potential to ensure you're creating and living a life you can be proud of. Envision the end of your life's journey. Dedicate time to writing down a memorial statement that captures the essence of the life you want to be living—the relationships you developed, accomplishments you achieved, moments of pride you fostered, and things you hope people would remember about you. Then, pledge to live that life *now.*

☀ ANTICIPATE

- ► Write a statement to describe your happiest self.

  - » *I am happiest when I am living out my purpose, investing in others, and taking time each day to appreciate the little things that make up my life journey. For me, this is building strong relationships with my spouse and my children. It's being a good friend who listens and encourages. It's recognizing that there are seasons of life where things are a grind, but those don't last forever. It's being a good leader who equips and empowers my team to become their best. It's when I finish the day knowing I made the world a slightly better place than it was before. This is when I'm thriving.*

CREATE YOUR TOUCHSTONE
(The Rules of Your Life)

We have spent the last chapters asking, "What rules?" Now it is time for you to write your own rules. But more than that, this final phase of the journey is not a black-and-white list of the dos and don'ts you've decided to follow. This is the creation of your Touchstone, the heart of your garden—and your life. It is a sanctuary to return to when you need reminding, reorienting, and reassuring that you're moving in the right direction on your path. The Touchstone will visually encapsulate the things that are significant for you, what brings you happiness, and what success will look like in your own life. It's a haven offering peace, comfort, and encouragement amid the implicit rules, expectations, and demands of life.

Guided by this simple mantra:

PLANT THE RIGHT SEEDS, AND THE
STRONG ONES TAKE ROOT.

OPPORTUNITIES BREAK THROUGH THE SURFACE
AND ARE STRENGTHENED BY CHALLENGES.

THEY KNOW WHERE TO FOCUS AND GROW
INTO A THRIVING, HEALTHY GARDEN.

Take the reflections you've crafted in the section above, and weave them into the pages that follow. This collection of your deep, true desires will create your Touchstone—your tangible guide around, through, and over the barriers currently on your road to success.

THE GOAL RULE

Start with you.

PLANT THE RIGHT SEEDS...
选籽播撒，筑梦芳华

Example:

» *I will invest in my gift of warmth and sense of humor to encourage others. Every time they engage with me, I will have made their lives better.*

» *I will use my ability to connect unconnected things and bring unique and innovative solutions to life for the people I serve.*

» *I will continue to be a learner, surrounding myself with positive voices and great books, so I can feed my sense of wonder and ideation.*

THE STRENGTH RULE

Lean into your strengths.

...AND THE STRONG ONES TAKE ROOT.

物竞天择, 良种根扎

Example:

» *Wonder and imagination are areas of strength for me. I feed my mind with good inputs, scheduling regular time for thinking and imagination, and look for ways to solve high-level problems.*

» *I look for ways to teach this to others so I can better understand my strength.*

» *I commit to reading three books per month so my mind is full of good thoughts and helpful information.*

THE OPPORTUNITY RULE

Focus on possibilities.

OPPORTUNITIES BREAK THROUGH THE SURFACE...

机遇助力, 破土生芽

Example:

» *I pursue opportunities that help fulfill my purpose of helping people bring their ideas to life.*

» *I look for ways to listen to others closely and apply my strength of strategy and clarity to their problems.*

» *I create opportunities to help me develop my strength of leadership by sending out a weekly text or email to people I want to mentor.*

THE LIMITS RULE

Thrive in challenges.

...AND ARE STRENGTHENED BY CHALLENGES.

风吹雨打, 生机勃发

Example:

» *I am stronger because I've faced my limits and surpassed them. Growing up as the child of a single mom, we didn't have a lot of opportunities. However, this made everything I worked to accomplish that much sweeter. When I was the first person from my family to walk across the stage and receive my college diploma, I thought of all the times my mom encouraged me to keep going when I wanted to quit, and I realized I will never give up on any of my dreams. My limits won't define me.*

THE EITHER-OR RULE

Integrate the essentials.

THEY KNOW WHERE TO FOCUS...

心无杂念, 形扬气佳

Example:

» *Family. My family is the most important thing in my life. I will always prioritize my family and make sure to build strong relationships with my spouse and my children. I want them to know they can always count on me.*

» *Health. I will always make room for exercise so I live a long and full life. For me, that means spending time jogging three to four times per week. I love to start my day with a brisk jog. It helps me clear my head and bring my best to the day ahead.*

» *Travel. I love to see new places. This means I will work hard so I can take one big trip each year and several smaller trips to new places. When I'm there, I will take lots of pictures, try new restaurants, and experience new cultures.*

» *Learning. It is essential for me to learn new things, so I will always look for new hobbies, skills, and challenges to keep me sharp and growing.*

THE HAPPINESS RULE

Enjoy the journey.

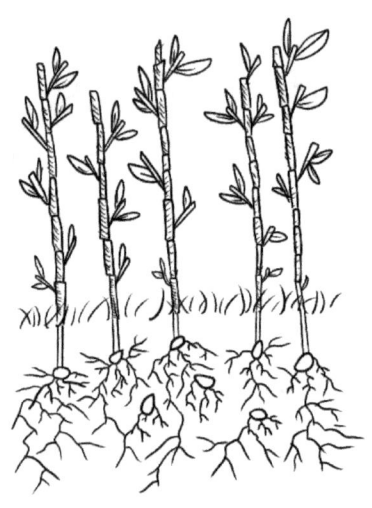

...AND GROW INTO A HAPPY, HEALTHY GARDEN.

成长为一个快乐、健康的花园

Example:

» *I am happiest when I am living out my purpose, investing in others, and taking time each day to appreciate the little things that make up my life journey. For me, this is building strong relationships with my spouse and my children. It's being a good friend who listens and encourages. It's recognizing that there are seasons of life where things are a grind, but those don't last forever. It's being a good leader who equips and empowers my team to become their best. It's when I finish the day knowing I made the world a slightly better place than it was before. This is when I'm thriving.*

Y our Touchstone is a living, breathing reflection of your authentic self and the garden you dream of cultivating with your life. Like a treasured Chinese garden, your Touchstone is meant to be revisited and reworked over time.

Don't close this book and let it gather dust on a shelf. Keep this labor of love you've done for yourself somewhere where you will see it often. Let it be a daily reminder to stay rooted in what truly matters to you. Use it as your compass when the implicit rules of life try to pull you off course.

Revisit this reflective journey again each year as you grow and evolve. Prune away the parts that no longer resonate while planting fresh seeds of new hopes and dreams. With each passing season, your garden will flourish more vibrantly, an embodiment of your ever-deepening self-awareness and happiness.

For now, let your Touchstone be a sanctuary of clarity amid life's chaos. Return to it whenever you need to feel grounded and focused on your true path. The way forward is no longer obscured by others' rules—your brilliantly personalized path stretches out before you, waiting to be nurtured and enjoyed with every step of this adventure that is called your life.

If you would like a printable copy of the last chapter of this book so you can fill in the Touchstone pieces and regularly revisit them in the years to come, simply visit WhatRulesBook.com/eleven.

ENDNOTES

Chapter 2

1. Oliver Wyman. "Making the Invisible Visible." Oliver Wyman . Accessed February 29, 2024.https://www. oliverwyman.com/content/dam/oliver-wyman/v2/ publications/2021/jan/Oliver-Wyman-Women-in-Leadership-Making-the-Invisible-Visible.pdf.

2. Field, Emily, Alexis Krivkovich, Sandra Kügele, Nicole Robinson, and Lareina Yee. "Women in the Workplace 2023." McKinsey & Company, October 5, 2023. https://www. mckinsey.com/featured-insights/diversity-and-inclusion/ women-in-the-workplace

3. Oliver Wyman. "Making the Invisible Visible." Oliver Wyman. Accessed February 29, 2024. https://www.oliverwyman.com/ content/dam/oliver-wyman/v2/publications/2021/jan/Oliver-Wyman-Women-in-Leadership-Making-the-Invisible-Visible. pdf.

4. Field, Emily, Alexis Krivkovich, Sandra Kügele, Nicole Robinson, and Lareina Yee. "Women in the Workplace 2023." McKinsey & Company, October 5, 2023. https://www. mckinsey.com/featured-insights/diversity-and-inclusion/ women-in-the-workplace

5. Smith, Morgan. "Burnout Is on the Rise Worldwide-and Gen Z, Young Millennials and Women Are the Most Stressed." CNBC, March 14, 2023. https://www.cnbc.com/2023/03/14/burnout-is-on-the-rise-gen-z-millennials-and-women-are-the-most-stressed.html.

6. Field, Emily, Alexis Krivkovich, Sandra Kügele, Nicole Robinson, and Lareina Yee. "Women in the Workplace 2023." McKinsey & Company, October 5, 2023. https://www. mckinsey.com/featured-insights/diversity-and-inclusion/ women-in-the-workplace

Chapter 3

7. Gladwell, Malcolm. David and Goliath: Underdogs, Misfits, and the Art of Battling Giants. New York, NY: Back Bay Books / Little, Brown and Company, 2015.
8. "Richard Branson Quote: 'Any Idea Can Be a Great Idea If You Think Differently, Dream Big and Commit to Seeing It Realized.'" Quotefancy. Accessed February 29, 2024. https:// quotefancy.com/quote/899381/Richard-Branson-Any-idea-can-be-a-great-idea-if-you-think-differently-dream-big-and.

Chapter 4

9. Oliver Wyman. "Making the Invisible Visible." Oliver Wyman. Accessed February 29, 2024. https://www.oliverwyman.com/content/dam/oliver-wyman/v2/publications/2021/jan/Oliver-Wyman-Women-in-Leadership-Making-the-Invisible-Visible.pdf.

Chapter 5

10. Team, Kwik. "How Goal-Setting Works in Your Brain." Jim Kwik, February 25, 2023. https://www.jimkwik.com/how-goal-setting-works-in-your-brain/#:~:text=No%20matter%20what%20your%20goals,whatever%20goal%20you%20strive%20towards.
11. "Your Desire to Get Things Done Can Undermine Your Effectiveness." *Harvard Business Review*, March 2016. Accessed January 27, 2024. https://hbr.org/2016/03/your-desire-to-get-things-done-can-undermine-your-effectiveness.
12. Gino, Francesca, and Bradley R. Staats. "Your Desire to Get Things Done Can Undermine Your Effectiveness." Harvard Business Review, March 22, 2016. https://hbr.org/2016/03/your-desire-to-get-things-done-can-undermine-your-effectiveness.
13. Yamato, Jen. "'Crazy Rich Asians': Gemma Chan Was on a Legal Track, Now She's a Movie Star." Los Angeles Times, August 10, 2018. https://www.latimes.com/entertainment/movies/la-et-mn-crazy-rich-asians-gemma-chan-20180810-story.html.

14. Randall, Lee. "Interview: Gemma Chan, Star of True Love." The Scotsman, May 27, 2012. https://www.scotsman.com/arts-and-culture/film-and-tv/interview-gemma-chan-star-of-true-love-1625556.

15. Ware, Bronnie. Bronnie Ware, February 25, 2022. https://bronnieware.com/blog/regrets-of-the-dying/.

Chapter 6

16. Smyth, Brenda R. "Be More Positive: Fight the Human Tendency to Focus on the Negative." Skillpath.com. Accessed February 29, 2024. https://skillpath.com/blog/positive-fight-natural-tendency-focus-negative#:~:text=The%20human%20brain%20has%20a,a%20mountain%20of%20good%20things.

17. Oliver Wyman. "Making the Invisible Visible." Oliver Wyman. Accessed February 29, 2024. https://www.oliverwyman.com/content/dam/oliver-wyman/v2/publications/2021/jan/Oliver-Wyman-Women-in-Leadership-Making-the-Invisible-Visible.pdf.

18. "Tom Rath Quote: 'People Have Several Times More Potential for Growth When They Invest Energy in Developing Their Strengths Instead of Cor...'" Quotefancy. Accessed February 29, 2024. https://quotefancy.com/quote/1537783/Tom-Rath-People-have-several-times-more-potential-for-growth-when-they-invest-energy-in.

19. Gallup, Inc. "CliftonStrengths." Gallup.com, February 2, 2024. https://www.gallup.com/cliftonstrengths/en/252137/home.aspx.

Chapter 7

20. "America's Richest Self-Made Women 2023." Forbes, June 1, 2023. https://www.forbes.com/self-made-women/?sh=1be11e7d6d96.

21. Pierson, David. "How I Made It: Panda Express' Billionaire CEO Dishes up a Stir-Fry Empire." Los Angeles Times, January 11, 2015. https://www.latimes.com/business/la-fi-0111-himi-panda-express-20150111-story.html.

Chapter 8

22. Rowling, J.K. "Harvard Commencement Address." J.K. Rowling, January 15, 2020. https://www.jkrowling.com/harvard-commencement-address/.

23. Middleton, Marc. "The Power of Persistence." Growing Bolder®, January 18, 2024. https://growingbolder.com/stories/the-power-of-persistence-2/.

24. "Simone Biles Makes History with Yurchenko Double Pike Vault at US Classic." The Guardian, May 23, 2021. https://www.theguardian.com/sport/2021/may/22/simone-biles-yurchenko-vault-us-classic.

Chapter 9

25. Mejia, Zameena. "Stanford Expert: One Key Question Can Help You Reduce Stress and Avoid Workplace Regret." CNBC, September 19, 2018. https://www.cnbc.com/2018/09/19/stanford-expert-ask-this-one-key-question-to-avoid-workplace-regret.html.

26. Field, Emily, Alexis Krivkovich, Sandra Kügele, Nicole Robinson, and Lareina Yee. "Women in the Workplace 2023." McKinsey & Company, October 5, 2023. https://www.mckinsey.com/featured-insights/diversity-and-inclusion/women-in-the-workplace.

27. Nooyi, Indra. "Parting Words As I Step Down as CEO." LinkedIn, February 24, 2019. https://www.linkedin.com/pulse/parting-words-i-step-down-ceo-indra-nooyi/.

28. "Conversation with PepsiCo CEO Indra Nooyi and David Bradley." YouTube, July 1, 2014. https://www.youtube.com/watch?v=KzLpryLUYsk.

29. Field, Emily, Alexis Krivkovich, Sandra Kügele, Nicole Robinson, and Lareina Yee. "Women in the Workplace 2023." McKinsey & Company, October 5, 2023. https://www.mckinsey.com/featured-insights/diversity-and-inclusion/women-in-the-workplace.

30. Gibson, Megan. "Study Finds People Who Ask for Advice Appear More Competent." Time, August 22, 2014. https://time.com/3158889/ask-for-advice-competent/.

31. Mejia, Zameena. "Stanford Expert: One Key Question Can Help You Reduce Stress and Avoid Workplace Regret." CNBC, September 19, 2018. https://www.cnbc.com/2018/09/19/stanford-expert-ask-this-one-key-question-to-avoid-workplace-regret.html.

Chapter 10

32 "One Third of Your Life Is Spent at Work." Gettysburg College. Accessed February 29, 2024. https://www.gettysburg.edu/news/stories?id=79db7b34-630c-4f49-ad32-4ab9ea48e72b#:~:text=The%20average%20person%20will%20spend%2090%2C000%20hours%20at%20work%20over%20a%20lifetime.

33. Shmerling, Robert H. "Why Life Expectancy in the US Is Falling." Harvard Health, October 20, 2022. https://www.health.harvard.edu/blog/why-life-expectancy-in-the-us-is-falling-202210202835#:~:text=For%20example%2C%20a%20baby%20born,in%20the%20US%20we%20live.

34. Martin, Emmie. "Pitbull and Richard Branson Agree on This Key Ingredient for Success." CNBC, June 18, 2017. https://www.cnbc.com/2017/06/16/pitbull-and-richard-branson-having-fun-is-key-to-success.html.

35. Miller, Mike, and Nina Biddle. "Kidnapping, Drugs and Scandal: Inside the Billionaire Getty Family's 'Curse.'" Peoplemag, December 25, 2017. https://people.com/movies/kidnapping-drugs-scandal-and-all-the-money-in-the-world-inside-the-getty-family-curse/.

www.ingramcontent.com/pod-product-compliance
Lightning Source LLC
Chambersburg PA
CBHW071322120626
46546CB00002B/405